Advance Praise for *The Sona Story*

'Mr Valliappa was a pioneer in the commercial real estate boom that was to sweep Bengaluru as it became a pre-eminent city for global development of software. Sona Towers, which he set up, was where Texas Instruments set up India's first remote satellite-based software development centre. Valliappa is unusual in the way he went beyond traditional manufacturing and trading, and seized the opportunities in high tech. This book gives us not only a glimpse of India's early IT days but also of a Chettiar businessman's journey of reinvention, and his unusual philosophies on life and work'

Nandan Nilekani
Co-founder and chairman, Infosys,
and founding chairman, UIDAI (Aadhaar)

'My first impression of . . . Mr C. Valliappa was created 34 years back as the landlord of the very fortuitous building Sona Towers. Titan made its beginnings in that place and I got to know Mr Valliappa better . . . His very polite manner and most reasonable negotiating style changed my impression from landlord to thoughtful businessman. Over the years I have seen him grow as he set up the Sona College of Technology, helped his sons incubate and build their businesses and, finally, was recognised by the global Nagarathar community for his contribution. I am sure this book about such an accomplished businessman and a good human will go a long way in helping budding entrepreneurs conduct themselves through life. I wish him even more success and growth'

Bhaskar Bhat
Former managing director, Titan

'In Mr C. Valliappa, we see a compassionate leader whose entrepreneurial skills have brought benefits to countless lives through IT, healthcare, education, textile mills, real estate and plantation. India needs more compassionate community leaders and entrepreneurs like Valliappa who excel in the art of enabling different strata of communities to create wealth and lead comfortable lifestyles. Valliappa is a shining example of a benevolent, spiritual-minded leader who has truly understood the art of giving back to the community and helping to establish peace, prosperity and social justice. This is an excellent book which is very well-written. Absolutely a must-read!'

Dr V.I. Lakshmanan
Chairman, Sringeri Vidya Bharati Foundation

'C. Valliappa's visionary approach, from transforming Sona Towers into Bengaluru's IT hub in the 1980s to crafting inspiring educational spaces, reflects his relentless pursuit of quality and innovation. His legacy of pushing boundaries and nurturing trust over decades is truly remarkable. A delightful and inspiring journey captured in *The Sona Story*!'

I.M. Kadri
Founder, IMK Architects,
and former sheriff of Mumbai

The Sona Story

THE SONA STORY

The Textile to Tech Journey of
Chettiar Industrialist C. Valliappa

CHITRA NARAYANAN

BLOOMSBURY
NEW DELHI • LONDON • OXFORD • NEW YORK • SYDNEY

BLOOMSBURY INDIA
Bloomsbury Publishing India Pvt. Ltd
Second Floor, LSC Building No. 4, DDA Complex, Pocket C – 6 & 7,
Vasant Kunj, New Delhi, 110070

BLOOMSBURY, BLOOMSBURY INDIA and the Diana logo
are trademarks of Bloomsbury Publishing Plc

First published in India 2025
This edition published 2025

Copyright © The Chockalingam Trust, 2025
Foreword copyright © Venu Srinivasan, 2025
'The Idea Behind the Book' copyright © Chocko Valliappa, 2025
'Roots and Routes' copyright © Thyagu Valliappa, 2025

The Chockalingam Trust has asserted their right under the
Indian Copyright Act to be identified as the Author of this work

All photographs courtesy of the Sona Group, unless mentioned otherwise

All rights reserved. No part of this publication may be reproduced or transmitted in
any form or by any means, electronic or mechanical, including photocopying,
recording or any information storage or retrieval system, without prior
permission in writing from the publishers

This book is solely the responsibility of the author and the publisher has had no
role in the creation of the content and does not have responsibility for anything defamatory or
libellous or objectionable

ISBN: HB: 978-93-61311-46-8; eBook: 978-93-61314-16-2
2 4 6 8 10 9 7 5 3 1

Typeset in Bembo by Manipal Technologies Limited
Printed and bound in India by Thomson Press India Ltd

To find out more about our authors and books visit www.bloomsbury.com
and sign up for our newsletters

Contents

Foreword by Venu Srinivasan — ix
Family Tree — xi
Inspiration — xiii
Key Milestones — xv
The Idea Behind the Book by Chocko Valliappa — xviii
Roots and Routes by Thyagu Valliappa — xxiii
Author's Note — xxvi

1. Under the Banyan Tree — 1
2. The Nagarathar Way: The Chettiar Heritage — 15
3. The Young Student Leader: College Days — 31
4. Valliappa, the Family Man — 41
5. Celebrating Eight Rich Decades — 56
6. Vyaparam: The 'Can Do' Spirit — 61
7. Seeding Knowledge: Institution Building — 85
8. Scaling Up and Making an Impact — 99
9. Dharmam: The Art of Giving — 108
10. The Divine Connection: Faith and Spirituality — 118
11. Love for Tamil — 126
12. Passion for Art and Architecture — 130
13. The Man and His Life Mantras — 138
14. Looking Ahead: Entrepreneurs, Not Inheritors — 146

Acknowledgements — 151
Notes — 153

Foreword

Until recently, there were very few business biographies being published in India. Thankfully, that trend has changed, and of late, there have been quite a few books chronicling the lives of entrepreneurs, businessmen and businesswomen who have had a hand in shaping India's extraordinary growth as a nation.

If India's economy expanded at a commendable rate of 6.7 per cent in 2024, even amid challenging external conditions, a large part is due to the sterling role played by our mid-sized organisations. At least 29 per cent of India's GDP comes from mid-sized entities, which have become the backbone of our economy. A lot of the work done by the low-profile family-owned groups in this sector, especially those from south India, has gone undocumented.

It is for this reason that *The Sona Story: The Textile to Tech Journey of Chettiar Industrialist C. Valliappa* is an important book. Not only does it chronicle the extraordinary life of a man I have had the pleasure of knowing, it also highlights the challenges of doing business in India, as well as the excellent opportunities open to intrepid entrepreneurs to seize upon in the country.

The book captures his story – one of perseverance, resilience and boundless faith – vividly. His trajectory from textiles to technology reflects not just his adaptability but also a vision to embrace change. His ability to reinvent himself in the face of adversity, whether by overcoming personal health challenges or by navigating business downturns, is inspirational. His

Foreword

leadership to the industry associations like the FKCCI at a young age remains legendary.

The book is also significant as it sheds light on the Chettiar community, known for its business acumen and god-fearing ways. What shines through is Mr Valliappa's belief in the intertwined nature of Vyaparam (business) and Dharmam (philanthropy). His initiatives, whether providing education to students in small towns through the Sona College of Technology, leading the Thiagarajar Polytechnic College to its pre-eminent position nationally, active participation in religious trusts and several community welfare initiatives, embody his philosophy that good deeds yield greater rewards.

I had the good fortune to participate in Mr Valliappa's eightieth birthday celebrations (sadabhishekam) in Salem in July 2024 where I listened to glowing tributes about him from leading academicians, industrialists, and political and religious leaders. And I found myself nodding in agreement, as these were characteristics I had noticed myself.

During our interactions, I have particularly noticed his humility, his ability to connect with people across all walks of life, and his commitment to family and community. His is a life that reflects the essence of leadership – one that inspires, guides and uplifts.

This book is not merely the story of a man but a testament to the power of dreams, resilience and values. I hope readers find it as inspiring and enriching as the life of Mr C. Valliappa itself.

Venu Srinivasan
Chairman Emeritus
TVS Motor Company Limited

Family Tree

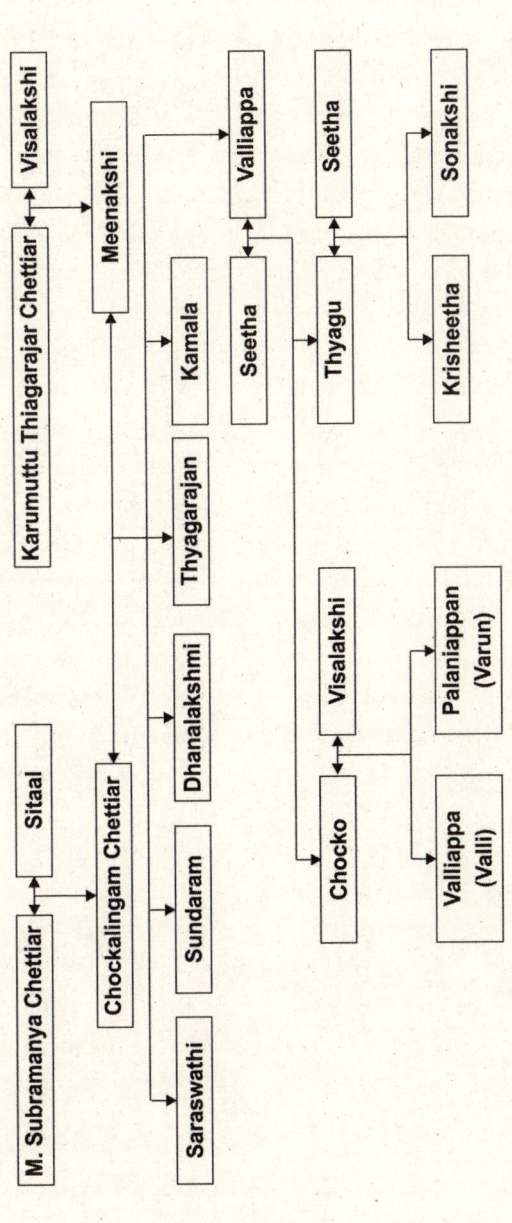

Inspiration
Everything for Everyone

நல்லாவின் பால் முழுதும் கன்றுக்கில்லை
நறும்பூவின் மணம் முழுதும் சோலைக்கில்லை
நெல்லாகும் கதிர் முழுதும் நிலத்துக்கில்லை
நிறைகின்ற நீர் முழுதும் குளத்துக்கில்லை
பல்லாரும் கனி முழுதும் மரத்துக்கில்லை
பண்ணரம்பு இசை முழுதும் யாழுக்கில்லை
எல்லாமே பிறர்க்குழைக்கக் காணுகின்றேன்
என் வாழ்வும் பிறர்க்குழைக்க வேண்டும்
வேண்டும்.

The milk of a good cow is not solely for its calf,
The fragrance of a flower is not solely for its bud,
The brightness of the sun is not just alone for the earth,
The rippling water is not confined for the use of the pond,
The fruit is borne not just for the benefit of the tree,
The sound of the strings is not purely for the musical instrument,
All these, I see, are meant to be shared with others,
So must my life be, always meant to be shared with others.

Va. Suba Manickanar
Former vice-chancellor
Madurai Kamaraj University

Key Milestones of the Sona Group

1922 – Karumuttu Thiagarajar sets up Meenakshi Mills, starts textile manufacturing in Madurai
1938 – Takeover of Rajendra Mills in Salem
1956 – Rajendra Mills B Unit started
1958 – Inception of Thiagarajar Polytechnic College (TPT)
1960 – Meena Finance begins operations
1963 – Foundation of Valliappa Textiles Bangalore unit in Ramanagara
1966 – Valliappa Textiles formally starts production
1972 – Yemmigoondi Estate in Coorg acquired
1973 – Sona Copper Sulphate started
1976 – Girls admitted to technical education for the first time in south India
1978 – Lalbagh Estate, a 1,000-acre coffee estate, purchased in Chikkamagaluru
1980 – Sona Synthetics mill started
1980 – Sona Towers Bhoomi Puja
1983 – Centre for Development of Telematics (C-Dot), a government enterprise, moves into Sona Towers. In the same year Valliappa Investment Private Limited locker division started
1984 – Texas Instruments, US, finds its home in India at Sona Towers. Marks setting up of first global IT research unit in India. Videsh Sanchar Nigam Limited (VSNL) started its office.
1990 – Spinwell Valliappa Private Limited started

Key Milestones of the Sona Group

1991 – Canada India Institutional Cooperation Project (CIICP) collaboration with Thiagarajar Polytechnic College

1991 – Sona Rajendra Spinners Private Limited incorporated in 1991 and the name is changed to Sona Valliappa Textiles Mills Private Limited in 2002

1996 – Valliappa Software Tech Park Incubation centre set up (Oracle, CISCO and Verifone find their first home in India at Sona Towers)

1997 – Sona College of Technology set up

1998 – Sona School of Management launched and the name changed to Sona School of Business Management in 2022

1999 – Pivoted spinning activities of Sree Valliappa Textiles to Sona Logistics

2000 – Vee Technologies is established

2000 – Vee Create (Engineering Services) set up

2001 – Vee Imaging Solutions started. Sona College of Technology starts research with Sona AROMA

2003 – Sona SPEED research and development division set up

2008 – Seetha Complex completed in Bengaluru

2010 – Vee Tech, US, launched in New York.

2015 – Play Factory, a sports and entertainment centre, established in Bengaluru

2017 – Launch of AI-driven online assessment platform, HireMee

2017 – Sona Arts and Science College started in Salem

2018 – Valliappa Foundation is set up

2019 – Sona Heights real estate project in Bengaluru

2019 – Sona Vistaas, a residential project, comes up in Bengaluru

2020 – Valliappa Public School starts in Salem

Key Milestones of the Sona Group

2020 – Anadhanam digital platform set up to solve nation-wide hunger through surplus food recycling
2021 – Sona Medical College of Naturopathy and Yoga Sciences in Salem
2022 – Mycelium Sona Biotech Private Limited set up in Salem
2021 – Vee Tech Acquires Meta-i Technologies (IT services company) set up
2022 – Sona Ayush Clinic started in Salem
2022 – Community radio Sona FM 89.6 launched
2022 – Sona Star launched
2023 – Vee Healthtek Private Limited launched
2023 – Sona Health Wellness Hospital starts its hospital and college at Salem
2024 – Courses for working professionals launched at Sona Technology Institute
2024 – Sona Accelerator and Incubation Foundation starts
2024 – Sona VT Towers and Estates, the infrastructure, wellness and construction wing of Sona VT, begins

The Idea Behind the Book

A Legacy of Inspiration

When we proposed a book on our father's life just short of his eightieth birthday, the idea excited and delighted him. But a minute or two later, he asked in his characteristically modest manner, 'Who will want to read about me?'

Although my father makes light of it, he has led a rich and exciting life. It has been a roller coaster ride for him in both life and health. Time and again he has bounced back, reinvented himself and been an inspiration to just about anyone who has met him.

I believe there is no man more positive and optimistic about the future than my father, C. Valliappa – an industrialist, an intrepid entrepreneur, a generous philanthropist, a Gandhian and a Chettiar to the core. His is a story – especially his philosophies on the way to do business and conduct oneself in life – that not only I but also his friends and colleagues believe needs to be shared.

As he is fond of saying – for a Chettiar, Vyaparam and Dharmam (Business and Philanthropy) are paramount. And these – a spirit of enterprise and business, and a sense of philanthropy – are ingrained in his very soul.

Like most Chettiars, he is a god-fearing person who observes all our traditions and rituals diligently. However, in many ways he is a rare Chettiar too – one who has ventured out of his comfort zone, moved out of traditional manufacturing and trading businesses and embraced technology and new ideas. From the traditional domain of textiles, the way he has journeyed into the world of tech is a fascinating story. Equally intriguing is his commitment to bringing education to the doorstep of students in remote tier-3 towns and making it inclusive.

My father's story begins from the small village of Poolankurichi in Chettinad before moving on to the salubrious town of Salem, where he made the Sona College of Technology a game-changer. From there he moved to the tech capital Bengaluru, where he first proved his mettle by running a successful textile business and then played a pivotal part in the IT revolution that propelled the city into a global league.

I have imbibed a lot from my father's philosophy on life and business. An incident that perfectly demonstrates my father's outlook on life occurred during a road trip from Salem to Bengaluru when I was a child. My father was driving a Fiat car – I remember it vividly – with five of us inside: my parents, my brother, an older cousin and I. Along the way, the car developed a puncture. We stopped and replaced it with the stepney, but soon after, another puncture brought us to a halt. My cousin volunteered to get the tyre repaired but took a long time to return.

As we waited under the hot sun, a man trudging along the road caught my father's attention. When my father asked where he was headed, the man replied he was walking to Bengaluru. Without hesitation, my father handed him a rupee – a significant amount in those days. My mother, ever practical, chided him, saying, 'The man didn't even ask and you gave him money.' My father's simple reply was, 'He's walking with such difficulty; I felt like helping him.'

Hours seemed to pass with no sign of my cousin, and we grew increasingly hungry. Then, a car stopped near us, and the driver asked about our predicament. Upon learning we were waiting for a tyre to be repaired, he insisted on sharing his food with us. As he drove away, my father turned to my mother and said, 'See, a good deed always begets another.'

This philosophy of compassion and generosity has been a cornerstone of my father's life, extending to his business practices. At the Valliappa Textile Mill on the Bengaluru–Mysuru highway, my father ensured that anyone facing an emergency on the road was brought in for treatment by the mill's on-site doctor. This simple act of kindness earned the company and my father immense goodwill and led to many lasting friendships. Additionally, the mill premises included separate accommodations for monks and other religious travellers to rest, cook and spend the night – a thoughtful gesture that reflected my father's values.

Some of my most vivid memories involve distinguished visitors to the mill. I still recall the 69th Kanchi Kamakoti Shankaracharya, Sri Jayendra Saraswathi, travelling by cycle rickshaw along the highway and stopping to rest at the mill. Another unforgettable moment was when Sri Sathya Sai Baba visited. At the time, I was curious – was he a godman, a magician or a saint? Sensing my thoughts, he looked directly at me and said, 'Why are you thinking so much? Just accept.' He then conjured a bracelet inscribed with 'Om' for me. Holding my hand, he advised, 'You're a student leader. People will tell you to enter politics. Don't – it's not for you.' As if that wasn't uncanny enough, he added, 'I can hear your father's Om chants every morning.' My father had only recently begun chanting while practising Hatha Yoga, a detail only he could have known. Before leaving, Baba manifested an emerald ring and placed it on my father's finger – a moment etched forever in my memory.

Resilience Through Challenge

My father's life has been anything but easy. He has faced numerous challenges in business, family and health. Stricken with a mild polio attack as a child, he developed a limp but never allowed it to slow him down. Even at seventy-six, I witnessed him climb ten uneven floors of the under-construction Sona College of Technology building – a feat that defied his condition. That this building, completed during the tumultuous COVID-19 years, now stands as the tallest in Salem is a testament to his unwavering determination and zeal. Aptly we named the building the Valliappa block.

One of the lowest points in his life came when his textile mill had to be shut down, leaving him with a mountain of debt. Another was a family dispute during which his brother and nephew prevented him from meeting his mother, a heartbreaking period for him. Yet, when his brother was hospitalised, he was the first to rush to his side.

Perhaps the most inspiring chapter of his life was when he lost his voice due to a health crisis. For a man who regularly presided over industry meets, chaired events and made countless work-related calls daily, this was a devastating blow. But even then, his attitude was, 'There is always a way ahead.' With sheer willpower and faith, his voice eventually returned – a testament to his resilience and optimism.

Lessons in Leadership

One of the most profound lessons I learned from my father came during a meeting with executives from Texas Instruments. I was just a 12th-grade rookie, sitting in the room as an observer. During the negotiations, a top executive of the company banged the table and raised his voice. My father, unflustered, calmly walked out, saying, 'You may be a top executive of a Fortune 500 company, but if you're negotiating with me, you need to be civil and human. Apologise, and we'll start again.' The executives apologised, and the agreement was

The Idea Behind the Book

signed. That day, I learned the importance of standing firm yet remaining humane.

It is no wonder that many of my father's business associates have remained loyal to him throughout his journey. His ability to balance toughness with compassion and professionalism with warmth speaks volumes about his management style and values.

Through it all – successes and failures, joys and sorrows – my father has remained steadfast in his belief in doing good, staying optimistic and moving forward. I hope for you, the reader, his life will be a source of endless inspiration, as it has been for me.

Chocko Valliappa
CEO and MD, Vee Technologies
Vice Chairman, Sona College of Technology

Roots and Routes

There is a certain romance and destiny to roads. The old Bengaluru–Mysuru Road has more than most. Legend has it that this winding road, with snaking twists and turns, once helped local rulers outwit invading armies as they knew the dangerous contours of the roads intimately.

This was also a road that in many ways shaped the destiny of my father, C. Valliappa, an unusual industrialist. When he was just twenty-three, my grandfather sent him to Bengaluru from Salem to prove his business acumen by setting up and managing the family textile factory in Hejala village, near Ramanagara, about an hour's drive from the city.

Back in the 1960s, when Sree Valliappa Textiles Limited was set up along the highway, the area was barren with nothing around for about 25 kilometres on either side. Do you remember the eerie rocky locale of the 1970s hit film *Sholay* where Gabbar Singh and his band of dacoits lived? This was in the vicinity.

And yet, under the able stewardship of my father, the mill quickly became a landmark on the road – a pitstop for politicians, bureaucrats and businessmen who would pause for a coffee and chat. The Valliappa Textiles signboard, written in Kannada, became a signpost for travellers on the road. A letter addressed to just 'Valliappa, Bangalore' with no more details would get delivered here – so famous was the mill.

Spirit of Adventure

The reason I brought in roads is because road trips define my father's outlook on life and business. He would think nothing of jumping into his car — a Fiat in the early days, followed by an Ambassador — and head off for a meeting from Bengaluru to Salem or to Chennai, Madurai, or his beloved coffee estate in Coorg, with his trusted driver Mariappan. He always kept his eyes peeled for opportunity.

Even today he clocks 700 kilometres a week and 2,500 kilometres a month on an average. At eighty, the car may have changed — a BMW now to have more room to flex his legs and provide more comfort — but the pace and indefatigable drive remains the same. You might see him in the morning in Bengaluru, in the late evening at Trichy with a stop in Salem for a simple meal and a quick meeting or two. He is seemingly tireless.

My mother, Seetha Aachi, with whom he consults for everything, has been a constant companion on these journeys and she thinks nothing of getting ready at a moment's notice. She is prepared for anything. If he mentions that there is a function in Salem the next day and suggests they go, she will be ready without a second thought.

Roots and tradition are as important to him as finding new routes. He is fiercely proud of his Chettiar heritage and follows all the rituals and rites of our tradition. Yet, he is extremely modern in his outlook and listens to all our ideas patiently. He never says no without giving an idea due consideration and is extremely flexible and quick to adapt.

People often assume that it is easier for a scion of a business family to achieve success, especially one hailing from the entrepreneurial Chettiar community, where business is in the blood. But it's by no means as smooth as perceived because circumstances, trends and policies change, the economic and social environments shift, and one has to keep evolving to stay ahead.

My father may be the third generation of an illustrious family that started business in the 1920s, but we know how the pressures on a third-generation entrepreneur are often far more than for a fresh start-up. Unless you reinvent and find new ways, it's tough. It's amazing how after every crisis my father has emerged stronger. When the textiles business became challenging, he pivoted and focused on education. He also spread out and diversified into everything from real estate to tech to agriculture – he is very savvy about the need to incorporate IT and tech in businesses, and you will find him bringing in new ideas into the plantation business too.

Even at the age of seventy-five, my father was setting up new businesses and new projects. He began his passion project, a low-rise residential development, with great zest, overseeing it personally and dreaming of scaling it up.

As such, my father's journey spanning from textiles to real estate to education to agriculture and tech is an inspirational one. He has seen it all from the days of the licence raj to the opening of the economy to the digital era to the pandemic (which he spent learning to use social media and other tools). Not only has he been a father to us, but he has also been a guide, guru and mentor. His journey holds invaluable lessons that continue to inspire us.

Thyagu Valliappa
Managing Director, Sona VT Towers and Estates
Vice Chairman, Sona College of Technology

Author's Note

I FIRST MET Mr Valliappa in November 2022 when his son Chocko Valliappa invited me to Poolankurichi, a tiny village in Chettinad, to celebrate the centenary of their ancestral home. During my visit I heard the history of the Chettiar community and was deeply fascinated. The thanksgiving celebrations held in the splendid Darbar hall of their palatial home exuded a wedding-like charm, but it was the warmth and hospitality of the Valliappas, who tended to each guest personally, that amazed me.

A few months later, when Chocko Valliappa broached the idea of a book about his father, I was immediately intrigued. What piqued my interest further was his account of how his father had tackled adversity time and again, emerging stronger each time. His transition – from managing a traditional textile manufacturing business to venturing into education and tech – sounded inspiring. The business journalist in me thought it was definitely a story that would resonate with family-owned businesses and B-school students alike. Another compelling motivation for my interest was the Sona Group's comparatively low profile; while a household name in Salem, they are not well known nationally. Here was a story that was eager to be told, especially as our regional satraps have had an incredible part to play in India's progress.

My first meeting with Mr Valliappa and his wife, Seetha Aachi, for the book took place at a bustling Bengaluru restaurant, where the noise made it difficult to hear them or

Author's Note

draw them into conversation. Their responses were rather stilted. For a moment, I felt a wave of despair, unsure of how I could encourage them to share their stories.

As I began meeting them in more familiar settings – at their Sona Towers office in Bengaluru, at their college campus in Salem, over dinner at Thyagu's Salem residence, at a lovely art-filled studio apartment in Bengaluru that they use as a guest house, at Chocko's beautiful villa – they opened up. The anecdotes began flowing like water, or perhaps more fittingly like the moringa pepper soup that Mr Valliappa seemed so fond of and got us hooked on too. Suddenly, my concern shifted from how to draw the stories out to how I could possibly fit them all. What should I include, and what should I leave out?

Given the Valliappas' demanding schedule and my own commitments, securing dates for meetings proved to be a challenge. For this, I must thank Sanjiv Kataria. This book, already delayed, would have faced further setbacks if Sanjiv had not stepped in, ensuring that meetings took place, diligently pursuing various people to confirm facts and verify incidents. His help has been absolutely invaluable.

The teachers at Sona College of Arts and Science – Anuradha, Pavithra and Preethi – were also instrumental in the writing process. Indeed, they started the whole thing off. They researched extensively, transcribed and helped with translations from Tamil. Mr Valliappa, an admirer of Tamil classical literature, would often quote a poem or phrase or idiom in the language, the nuances of which would be lost on me. A personal highlight has been the way he introduced the world of Thirukkural couplets and their teachings on virtue, love and wealth.

As I spent more time with Mr Valliappa, I came to appreciate his gentleness, his old-world charm, his warmth and interest in everyone's welfare and his generosity. Oh yes, there is steel in his core, but it is sheathed in an armour of bonhomie.

Author's Note

His sons had told me about his indefatigable energy, but I soon came to experience it firsthand. I would be ready to be pack up and leave by six, but he would show no signs of tiredness. On one occasion, despite having a busy day, he suggested meeting us (the Sona teachers, Sanjiv and me) at 6 p.m. The meeting continued through dinner and went on till 11 p.m.

I found out that though he may appear to be a man of few words, his words carry a lot of weight. His wit is dry and subtle, and he uses humour with finesse to chide someone without causing offence. Nothing seems to frazzle him or stress him. The trick, he said, is to always look at the bright side.

He encouraged us to meet as many people as we could for the book to capture a wide range of perspectives and avoid making it a hagiography – but everyone had only good things to say. The goodwill he commands, even from passing acquaintances, is remarkable.

Each visit to Salem or Bengaluru would uncover something new – a new pet project, another expansion or a compelling opportunity he had spotted. Once he had made up his mind, the Sona Group chairman lost no time executing his plans. For instance, he once mentioned he had found a spot for a new building on the campus, and on our next visit, we found the architects already on the job. This made writing the book a bit difficult, because the Sona story is far from complete. Not only is the chairman's vision grand, but his children are also brimming with innovative ideas. A sequel will surely be needed soon.

I must also make special mention of the Bloomsbury team. The affable Mr Krishan Chopra, who bowled us over at our first meeting at a cosy tearoom in South Delhi and was ever encouraging. Mekhala Moorthy, who very efficiently executed the project, Jaishree Ram Mohan who lent a sympathetic ear whenever I was stuck, and Krittika Gogoi who edited the manuscript ruthlessly making it a crisp read.

1

Under the Banyan Tree

ON THE LEAFY, tree-lined Millers Road, barely a kilometre from the majestic Vidhana Soudha in Bengaluru, stands a tall, white building without a nameplate. Its beautiful jaali (lacy lattice work) facade has an old-world charm to it. A large banyan tree stands guard near the gate. Elegant yet unassuming, this is Sona Towers, which houses the corporate office of the Valliappa Group, a textiles-to-education-to-technology conglomerate. It holds a special place in India's glorious information technology (IT) story. It is here that India's software, telecom and consumer revolution story took off.

The reception area has elements of a Chettinad home. The flooring – made with vibrant and exquisite Athangudi tiles – stands out. Lending great character to the ceiling is an ancient wooden door that once graced the Valliappas' 140-year-old ancestral Chettinad home in Poolankurichi, now repurposed as an artefact. Behind the reception desk is a stunning tree-of-life sculpture in silver.

The museum vibes continue into the conference room, where the legs of the table are wooden pillars transplanted from Chettinad. But the centrepiece is a framed photograph circa 1985 of a bullock cart bringing a satellite dish to the door of Sona Towers hanging on the wall. Nobody remembers why a bullock cart, rather than a truck, was used to tow the satellite, but the picture is symbolic of India's leapfrogging from the bullock cart age to the information age.

At that time Sona Towers had just been set up, a futuristic building for that era, the development of which was painstakingly overseen by C. Valliappa, a textile magnate, who was venturing into commercial real estate for the first time. The only construction experience he had was of building two state-of-the-art textile mills in Ramanagara, on the outskirts of Bengaluru, with some unique features like pillarless halls with a concrete roof, designed by a French architect.

Among the early milestones in India's IT story is the entry of the US multinational company (MNC) Texas Instruments (TI) into the country. And it was in Sona Towers that TI set up its software design centre. Sona Towers was the first private building in Bengaluru to install and use a satellite dish with uplinking facilities for all the IT companies there, with the organisation tasked with providing international communication services – Videsh Sanchar Nigam Limited or VSNL (then called Overseas Communication Services) – setting up an earth station here. Several black-and-white pictures of the executives of TI, along with then Karnataka chief minister Ramakrishna Hegde, then US Ambassador John Gunther Dean, TI India's first head, Charlie Simon, and Valliappa grace the walls.

Sona Towers went on to become the incubation hub for a host of multinationals such as Verifone, Oracle, Cisco and ANZ IT, igniting the IT boom in Bengaluru. The Centre for Development of Telematics, popularly known as C-DOT, had chosen Sona Towers as its corporate office. And it was from here that the C-DOT exchanges transformed the telecom landscape. Thus, in a sense, Sona Towers also catalysed telephony in India. The likes of A.P.J. Abdul Kalam, N. Vittal and Sam Pitroda, all passed through the doors of the building as India's IT revolution and telecom boom took place.

Valliappa's eldest son, Chocko, remembers an event at Delhi's Taj Palace where Infosys co-founder and technocrat Nandan Nilekani was onstage delivering a keynote. Pointing to Chocko in the audience, Nilekani said, 'There is the man whose dad was the father of the IT revolution.'

Recalling those heady days, Nilekani says, 'The achievement of Mr Valliappa was he was the first entrepreneur to work with a global multinational like Texas Instruments to put up India's first remote software development centre using satellites.'

Nilekani describes how, in the 1980s, Bengaluru, which had a long tradition of pioneering new technology (it was here that India's first electric pole was set up in 1905), had just begun to embrace software development. The IT hardware story had already taken off, with companies like DCM Data Products, ECIL and Patni Computers, among others. The new buzz was around software.

Nilekani says, 'It was the latest cycle of technology in Bengaluru. And we led the cycle as Infosys had just moved to Bengaluru in 1983. The arrival of TI, the first multinational software development company in India, had its own impact. The fact that an American company from Texas was willing to come here gave a psychological boost to software development in the city. TI was a pioneer in remote development of software. The notion that sitting in an office in Sona Towers on Millers Road you could write software for a company in Dallas was a leap forward. There was an executive called V. Mohan Rao in TI who was involved in the move.'

The IT czar says the earth station in Sona Towers helped unlock a government programme called Software Technology Parks of India (STPI). 'STPI is one of the most successful programmes of the government as it invested in buying more earth stations. These were under the Ministry of Electronics. One came up in Electronic City in Bengaluru and further fuelled the boom in software,' he says.

The Sona Story

Valliappa recalls the excitement in Bengaluru those days, and how the whole ecosystem was geared towards enabling software development. In 1984, the new computer policy was laid out. Valliappa says, 'Rajiv Gandhi arrived with the promise of taking India on to the information highway. He wrote to IT companies within the Fortune-500 list, inviting them to a breakfast with him. TI was the first to accept that invitation. The CEO of TI flew over to India and met with Rajiv, who promised a red carpet welcome and easy clearances at Customs.'

Texas Instruments settled on Bengaluru as the city was home to institutions such as the Indian Institute of Science (IISc), the Indian Institute of Management Bangalore (IIM-B) and Bharat Electronics Limited. After prospecting other buildings, TI chose Sona Towers because of its structural strength and because Valliappa promised to provide all the infrastructure they sought, including reliable power. In addition, TI had asked for wind maps of buildings because it was putting up a satellite and the load of the satellite was unknown. 'We were the only ones who had a wind map,' says Chocko.

It was by sheer providence that Sona Towers had a wind map. As Chocko explains, when his father was building Sona Synthetics in 1965, his grandfather, who had built a 120-foot-span building earlier, challenged him to construct one with a wider span. 'My father accepted the challenge and went to the IISc, where he obtained the wind map for a space frame truss structure.' So he got a wind map done for his next building too, Sona Towers. As Nilekani points out, 'An earth station had to be lifted all the way to the top of the building and the building had to be strong enough for that.'

Writing for *The Week* in 2021, Montek Singh Ahluwalia, who was special secretary to then prime minister Rajiv Gandhi, recalls, 'When Texas Instruments decided to set up its first research and development facility abroad in Bangalore, the policy in place at the time did not allow them to operate a dedicated satellite facility to allow seamless connectivity with Houston. Rajiv took a personal interest in ensuring that this problem was satisfactorily resolved. The subsequent success of the TI venture set the trend for other multinationals to set up similar ventures in India.'[1]

Srini Rajam, founder of Ittiam Systems and former managing director (MD) of Texas Instruments, India, recalls how Sona Towers was built with a futuristic approach. 'TI took the lead in asking for world-class infrastructure. The Sona Group had a very good customer orientation. They very well understood the requirements of their customers and provided everything we asked for,' he says.

In the early 1980s, there was a horrific accident in Bengaluru when Gangaram building, a seven-storey structure that was under construction on Subedar Chhatram Road, collapsed, resulting in several deaths. This led to a stay on all commercial constructions for some months.

The Sona Group was first to be granted permission, thanks to the impressive Sona Synthetics textile plant it had constructed, whose structural engineering was done by C.R. Narayana Rao with the help of the IISc.

Valliappa asked Narayana Rao to recommend an architect to design Sona Towers. Rao suggested two Mumbai-based architects. Valliappa travelled to Mumbai and first met a well-known Parsi architect. The architect did not spend much time with Valliappa and left it to his team to take down the specifications. The following day was spent at IMK Architects, where the founder, I.M. Kadri, showed Valliappa multiple options over the course of many hours. Valliappa, who loves building long-term business relationships, had met a kindred spirit in Kadri. To date, IMK Architects designs all new structures for the Sona Group, enjoying the status of family architects. In those days, Kadri used to proudly say, we work with just five clients and Valliappa is one of them.

Valliappa wanted no compromise on quality and spared no expense to make the building strong and secure, exceeding the normal specifications. It had an earthquake-resistant foundation. It used two-way slabs without any beams. The construction cost shot up from ₹250 per square foot to ₹350 per square foot. 'The fact that we went over and above the specifications was what bought in TI. The authorities were so pleased they began citing Sona Towers as an example of a model building,' says Chocko.

TI also insisted on continuous power supply and Valliappa was enterprising enough to get a dedicated power line from Raj Bhawan and fit two UPSs of 250 kVA each as well as a 500 kVA generator in the building. Today a 250 kVA UPS could fit under a chair. Those days two of those UPSs and the generator occupied an entire basement.

Nilekani acknowledges the pioneering infrastructure. 'There was a certain level of infrastructure that had not yet been seen and the whole ecosystem swung into action to support Valliappa,' he says, pointing out that there was a general recognition and excitement in Bengaluru that it was an important step forward in establishing a new industry.

How did Infosys view the entry of TI? 'We welcomed it as it sort of validated and legitimised what we were saying. That Bengaluru, and India, was a great place for software development,' Nilekani says.

In those early days many architects of Indian IT visited Sona Towers, and Valliappa would chat with them. A frequent visitor was the bureaucrat N. Vittal, who was then Secretary, Department of Electronics, and a great nurturer of Indian IT. Valliappa recalls how Vittal would often come up with out-of-the box solutions to help out the nascent

IT industry. For instance, when TI grew its staff, it rented additional space in a building a kilometre away, where it was taking too long to install a dial-up connection. Vittal hit upon the ingenious idea of a point-to-point solution with a wireless LAN setup, and it worked.

Says Valliappa, 'I always remember how Vittal used to say, Bengaluru was a city of parks once, now it is a city of software parks too.'

Another memory from those days is of being awakened by a call at 2 a.m. from an official of the Indian Space Research Organisation (ISRO). In the late 1980s, ISRO relied on satellite launches from French Guiana. Apparently, the communication lines were being overworked just before a launch, and the call was to request Sona Towers to be on standby to provide an additional line if needed.

Consumer Revolution

Sona Towers is also where the Titan saga began, marking the start of the consumer revolution in India. The famous watch company from the house of Tatas was incubated as a start-up here. At the time of signing of the lease, Xerxes Desai, the charismatic first managing director of Titan Company, told Valliappa that he could not pay the market rent as the company was a start-up. Valliappa wondered aloud how a Tata company could bargain like that. 'That is why we are Tatas,' quipped Desai.

Valliappa thought over it and agreed. He knew Titan would not remain a start-up long. 'When you declare your first dividend, the rent must be raised ten per cent,' he told Desai. A few years later, much to Valliappa's delight, even without a reminder, the Tata group company honoured the promise. Valliappa says this was a first-of-its-kind agreement.

Valliappa was also a good judge of character and only did business with those in whom he sensed integrity and with whom he saw promise of a flourishing, long-term relationship. 'I like to bargain and negotiate because I don't want to be cheated. But at the same time, I weigh the long-term benefits before making a decision,' he explains.

Therefore, he refused to take on many tenants right after the building was ready even though a huge loan had to be paid off. He did not like either the terms offered or the business principles. For instance, a famous restaurant chain wanted to take up 7,000 square feet, but during the meeting the restaurateur boasted about the number of chickens that were killed a day to serve the chain's fabled butter chicken dish. Valliappa, a rare vegetarian Chettiar because of his family's close association with Mahatma Gandhi, turned down the tenant. Similarly, he showed the door to another company's representatives who wanted to pay less rent as they refused to take into consideration the skirting on the mosaic, common areas and toilets while calculating the per foot area. 'These potential tenants, Karnataka Industrial Investment Development Corporation, were valued associates of mine in the textiles business, but I did not budge because if you compromise for one, you would have to for others,' says Valliappa. In those days hardly any building provided a super built-up space with so many frills and bells and whistles – the norm was to give a bare space and let the tenant furnish it. In that sense Sona Towers was ahead of its time yet again.

Even with TI, Valliappa was adamant that he would allow them to take the building only if the terms were met. 'Although here was a big MNC, my father was not at all subservient but very firm. During the initial negotiations, when he refused to budge, one of the exasperated TI executives banged the table. My father just said, please don't bang on the table, and in soft tones explained his position. He completely disarmed them,' says Chocko.

Valliappa was passionately involved in the making of the Sona Towers building and its maintenance. 'Architecturally, there were two things important in the building,' says Rahul Kadri, principal architect at IMK Architects and son of I.M. Kadri. 'It had flat slabs. It was the very first time in Bengaluru that a building had been set up with flat slabs, and with no beams. This provided a clean, open space, without any barriers.'

The second thing, says Kadri, was that a beautiful jaali facade was created which allowed a soft quality of light to filter in. 'We worked on two things – how do you provide maximum uninterrupted space. How do you provide good quality light to penetrate the building? And we achieved both.'

In the course of constructing the building, Valliappa and I.M. Kadri, who was at one time the sheriff of Bombay, developed a great rapport. If Valliappa wanted an outstanding building, Kadri was equally eager to create an exemplary structure.

For its time, the building was really grand – the bannister was made of cast brass, which was fairly expensive, but it lifted the tone of the building. While the facade was low-key, much like its owner, it was a stylish, solid space.

The interiors were also state-of-the-art, recalls Anand Joseph, whose fledgling company Talin won the contract to do the office furniture in the building. It was the first building with modular furniture. TI had imported its workstations from the US. These were Haworth furniture. When Valliappa saw it, he told Joseph to execute something that was as good and also modular.

Says Joseph, 'One of the tenants – Meritor – said, you must do the interior, but if there is a delay, there will be a penalty.

To which Mr Valliappa retorted that if there was a penalty for delay, then for early completion there should be a bonus. We actually got the bonus.'

The building was lovingly built with great attention to detail and so took a few years to complete. But when it was completed, it not only drove growth for the Valliappa family but also allowed a whole new, upcoming industry – the software and IT services – to flourish. Given the ban on construction, the newly formed IT companies were struggling to find office space in Bengaluru. 'The timing of Sona Towers was just right,' says Valliappa modestly. In business, timing matters a lot, he adds.

Both Valliappa and the architect were adamant that no tree was to be cut in the making of the building. A banyan tree is prominent by the gate and therein lies another story. The tale goes that Karumuttu Thiagarajar Chettiar, the celebrated ancestor of the Valliappa clan, would often buy land attracted by the trees on it and would get especially sentimental if he spotted a banyan tree. And this credo has been followed by his scions, though Valliappa throws in a caveat, 'You may covet a piece of land, but only if it is fated will that piece of land come to you.'

Decades later, the mature banyan tree at the entrance symbolises the traditional welcome to thousands of people every day.

Valliappa also believes that if a piece of land is destined to remain with you, it just will not be sold. A case in point, he says, is the property he had acquired in Raja Rajeshwari Nagar in Bengaluru that he was trying hard to dispose of. 'I had set my selling price at five hundred rupees per square foot. One man came up to four hundred and ninety-five rupees per square foot, but refused to climb up to five hundred rupees, and the talks ended there. For just five rupees per square foot, the talks failed.' Today, the Seetha apartment complex stands on it, built by Valliappa. It was destined to stay with us,' says Valliappa philosophically.

A Sheltering Canopy

The Sona Group logo is a banyan tree, with which the promoters strongly identify. 'A banyan tree is old, has heritage, and it has many offshoots. When the branches reach the ground, it promptly puts down roots to another tree. It also provides shelter to many. The banyan tree is our legacy,' explains Chocko. The banyan is known for its longevity and in Hindu mythology is revered for its leaf being the resting place of Lord Krishna.

Chocko points out the tree's similarities with Sona Group, which started in textiles, branched into education, putting down very deep roots in the knowledge field, and spread to construction, technology, outsourced services, agriculture, coffee plantations and entertainment. And there are similarities with the Valliappa family itself, which hailed from Chettinad and spread out to Madurai, to Salem and then on to Bengaluru, followed by the US, Singapore and the Philippines, putting down roots everywhere they went. 'My father believes that one has to keep one's community traditions intact but at the same time assimilate into whichever setting you are in. He learnt the local language and speaks Kannada like a native,' says Chocko. He even dropped the letter n in his name to be seen as a local. Valliappan is a Tamil name, while Valliappa is close to Belliappa, a local Kannada, Coorgi name.

For the man who built Sona Towers, the building changed his destiny in many ways. Like all major industrialist families in India, the Valliappa family too had started in textiles. Soon after his graduation, Valliappa, the youngest son of his parents, joined the family textile unit in Salem and, two years later, was sent to Bengaluru to expand the textile empire, as his father, Chockalingam Chettiar, wanted help. Heeding a call from the government to industrialists to build India's social capital, the family had also forayed into education to skill young talent, and in parallel that enterprise was expanding, occupying the time and energies of Chockalingam Chettiar.

The real estate project happened by accident. The plot on Millers Road had been bought by Valliappa's father in the early 1970s to build the family home. When the Valliappa family moved to Bengaluru in the 1960s, they lived on Lavelle Road on rent, near the Bangalore Club, and then on Brunton Road, a two-minute walk from Brigade Road.

'When we took the house on a five-hundred-rupee per month rent in Bengaluru, there was no fan in it. We did not need it, though we got a few installed,' says Valliappa. 'Today, can you imagine a Bengaluru home without an AC?' he exclaims, ruing the climate change.

'Lavelle Road was where the wave of businesspeople coming from Tamil Nadu to Bengaluru made their base,' says Thyagu, the younger son of Valliappa, recalling those halcyon days when a constant stream of visitors from Tamil Nadu came to their home and launched into stimulating discussions on business opportunities.

But it was decided to make the family home in Koramangala, where Valliappa had bought land in 1979. Since Koramangala was just a village then, his grandfather joked that Valliappa must have bought the land thinking it was closer to Salem. And so the Millers Road land was put to use in a commercial real estate project.

Says Nilekani, 'Mr Valliappa was a critical pioneer in the commercial real estate boom that was to sweep Bengaluru, which became a pre-eminent place for global development of software. These software centres were housed in real estate projects built by Prestige, Manayata and Bagmane, to name a few. But the story began with Sona Towers.'

Indeed, M.R. Jaishankar, real estate mogul and Brigade Group's founder, once told Thyagu that for an aspiring builder like him the Sona Towers building was a benchmark in those early days.

Although the Valliappa family engaged in a few more real estate residential projects after that, their focus switched to education and their technology start-ups. However, that first experience of building Sona Towers and the heady thrill of successful execution of the project stayed in Valliappa's mind and at the age of seventy-five, he plunged into another passion real estate project – the Sona Vistaas residential township in Begur, matching wits with Rahul Kadri and his team.

Life had come full circle.

Constant Reinvention

Looking back, the one thread in Valliappa's business journey, says Chocko, is 'reinvention'. If one door shut, he would open another. And he is ever open to opportunities – the latest being space tech.

Valliappa points out how he was always futuristic in his business ventures. He started Sona Synthetics when nobody had yet bet on polyester. He was ahead of the curve on the fabric. Then he introduced open-end spinning, a new technique in the mills, even as others were still in wait and watch mode. 'We also went into knitting and exports in a big way very early on,' he recalls.

On his own steam, independent of the businesses he inherited from his father, Valliappa founded many ventures including Sona Synthetics Private Limited, Sona Valliappa Textiles Private Limited, Valliappa Investments Private Limited,

Valliappa Software Technological Park Private Limited, Sona Vistaas and Sona Coffee Plantations Private Limited. (Businesses that did not work for various reasons include Sona Copper Sulphate and Valliappa Lockers.)

He also founded Sona SPEED (Sona Special Power Electronics and Electric Drives), a research and development (R&D) division working in specialised motors, which has been collaborating with ISRO for years.

And, of course, he grew the family's Sona Educational Institutions, adding more colleges and schools to the ones built by his father and grandfather. The Sona College of Arts and Science is his baby, as is the Sona Valliappa Public School.

He has also been an inspiring force in his sons' ventures, encouraging Chocko to set up Vee Technologies, and Thyagu to set up Sona Star, Sona Ayush, TrackMySona and other ventures.

The Sona Group has also ventured into biotech with the founding of Mycelium Sona Biotech (MSB). The Sona Group inaugurated its first laboratory in Salem in association with Australian company Mycelium.

As Nilekani, who is Valliappa's neighbour in Koramangala, points out, 'He is an unusual Chettiar. To move out of the traditional businesses and spot opportunities in high tech and reinvent himself – that's quite a story!'

It has been a journey of evolution and progression – keeping pace with the contexts of the time. But the roots all go back to a little village in Chettinad, and the genes of a business- and philanthropy-oriented community.

2

The Nagarathar Way: The Chettiar Heritage

EVERY TIME THERE is a wedding or any significant celebrations in the family — milestone birthdays or anniversaries – the Valliappas make their way to Poolankurichi, a tiny village in the Sivaganga district of Tamil Nadu, where their palatial ancestral home is opened up, and plays host to festivities.

The serene little village has 900-odd homes and about 4,000 people living in it. The peaceful hamlet with hills in the distant background and dotted with temples has an air of quiet prosperity. Shops abound and every amenity you would get in a city seems available. There are several big homes here, though many have a disused, neglected air.

But the Valliappa home wears a fresh coat of paint and is in pristine condition. Over a hundred years old, Lakshmi Vilas, strategically located near the Poolankurichi bus stand (jokingly referred to as Poolankurichi downtown), has been restored lovingly to its old glory and is opulent beyond imagination, with checkerboard-tiled floors, decorative wooden pillars, painted ceilings and walls that tell stories through heritage artworks. An incredibly large and heavy key (so big it once created consternation at the airport security check where it was mistaken for a weapon) opens the statement teak door which, even after a century, is so well-oiled that it opens smoothly. The heritage house was restored in 2022 on its hundredth anniversary when colourful centennial celebrations took place, with guests coming from far and near. The two-day celebrations were marked with dance and musical performances, and stories and reminiscences were shared about the home and old Chettiar traditions.

In July 2024, the mansion came alive again when Valliappa's eightieth birthday was celebrated here with pomp and glory.

The Valliappas of the Sona Group belong to the prosperous Nagarathars or Nattukottai Chettiar community. Fiercely proud of their heritage, they hold on to their traditions and rituals, and their ancestral homes speak of a wealthy past even as they embrace modern business practices.

Considering their minuscule numbers — by some estimate there are barely 80,000–100,000 families — the Nagarathars wield disproportionate influence in India's business firmament. Hardworking, humble and god-fearing, with traditional values, the clan is small in size but big in stature. The community has left a strong, silent imprint on several industries — from textiles to manufacturing to banking to fertilisers and films — and contributed in a big way to education.

Jawaharlal Nehru specially mentions the community in *The Discovery of India*: 'The Chettys of Madras have been leaders in business, and banking especially, from ancient times. The word "Chetty" is derived from the Sanskrit word "Shreshthi", the leader of a merchant guild. The common appellation "Seth" is also derived from Shreshthi. The Madras Chettys have not only played an important part in south India, but they spread out all over Burma, even in the remote villages.'[1]

According to some sources, Chettiar is derived from the ancient Tamil term 'etti', which was bestowed on merchants by Tamil rulers.

In ancient times, the Chettiars — who were Vaisyas of the Lunar race — lived in Sandhyapuri in Naganadu, an area that, in the present day, is on the border between Andhra Pradesh and Tamil Nadu. They traded precious stones. Around 2897 BCE, a large number of them left Naganadu as they could not bear the harassment of the king, who taxed them heavily. They moved to a place near Kanchipuram, where the king welcomed them, gifting them land to build temples. The Chettiars who remained in today's Andhra bear the surname Chetty. Those who moved came to be known as Nattukottai Chettiars. In Kanchipuram they continued to trade in precious stones and lived there till 790 BCE.

In 789 BCE, the Kanchipuram king Prathaparasa began imposing fines and punishment and the Chettiars moved again, this time to the port city of Kaveripoompattinam, which we know today as Poompuhar, and settled down on the banks of the Cauvery. This was the capital of the mighty Chola empire and a flourishing town with the river Cauvery meeting the sea. Here the Chettiars grew in stature and power. Manu Needhi Cholan (260 BCE to 161 BCE) gave them three rights – one, that they could play a part in the coronation of the kings; two, that they could have a flag of their own (with a lion as emblem); and three, that they could have golden kalasams (ritualistic pots) in their homes. They lived here for nearly 1,400 years until a natural calamity struck and the port city was submerged in a deluge. This led to their last migration – to the Sivaganga region around 707 CE.[2]

There are different versions of the reason the Chettiars moved to this district. One is that they wanted to stay in a dry place, as Kaveripoompattinam witnessed frequent floods. Sivaganga region is very arid, but even here they built their houses on raised platforms.

Another version says that Soundaraja Pandiyan, who ruled over this region, approached the Chola king Rajabhusha Cholan requesting him to spare a few good citizens. The Chettiars were agreeable, but as they did not want to be split up they moved en masse.³

The Chettinad region, as the area in Sivaganga eventually came to be called, is spread over 1,550 square kilometres and initially comprised ninety-six villages (it has reduced to around seventy-six now). The Nattukotai Chettiars have nine divisions, demarcated based on nine temples in the area, and every Chettiar family (known as pulli) is attached to one of these nine temples. The nine clan temples are Pillayarpatti, Ilayathangudi, Illupakudi, Iraniyur, Mathur, Nemam, Surakudi, Vairavanpatti and Velangudi. The Valliappa family is attached to Pillayarpatti.

The first houses that the Nattukotai Chettiars built in this area were fairly simple, indicating that the community was not very wealthy. They mostly traded rice, salt and pearls.

Gradually the Chettiars progressed to moneylending and earned renown as financiers. Around the 1850s, the intrepid community members began making voyages to Myanmar (erstwhile Burma), Sri Lanka (erstwhile Ceylon) and Malaysia (erstwhile Malaya) and got into timber, rice, tea, coconut and rubber plantations as well as tin factories, making big fortunes.

S. Rajagopal, retired senior epigraphist, Tamil Nadu Archaeology Department, said in a paper presented at the French Institute of Pondicherry that Nattukotai Chettiars were salt traders in the seventeenth century.⁴ By the eighteenth century, some individuals had extended their business operations to cover pearl, rice and cloth trade in Sri Lanka, and rice and wheat trade in Kolkata. Wherever they went, they carved a business presence. But despite their wide travels, the Chettiars never lost their community traits – big on tradition, they preserved their culture, cuisine, clothing and rituals. The Chettinad checked saris continue to be popular and industrialist families from the community have revived textile-weaving units in the area.

The Nagarathar Way: The Chettiar Heritage

Quality and ethics matter for Nagarathars, says A. Alagappan, a prominent Chettiar and educationist and a friend of the family. He says the Valliappa family has this trait in abundance.

As the wealth of the community grew, it began to reflect in the Chettiar dwellings back home. Materials imported from various countries – teak from Myanmar, tiles from Italy, chandeliers from Belgium, artefacts from Vietnam and Cambodia – were used in the opulent homes that came up. However, many of the important architectural features of the original modest homes were preserved, for instance, the east–west orientation, the outer veranda or thinnai supported by columns, an inner courtyard open to the sky with similar columns, around which are the rooms.

Over time, as they became even wealthier and began appreciating the fine arts and culture of the places they travelled to, it began to show in their homes. The walls were now embellished with elaborate paintings, the doors had elaborate carvings, the tapering columns in the thinnai were made of teak set on fluted granite bases and topped by ornate wooden brackets, false ceilings were made of wood in criss-cross patterns and adorned with breathtaking paintings in some halls.

Valliappa's home has many of these features. You enter through the doorway into the thinnai and from thence into a central durbar hall that is the majestic centrepiece of the house, whose embossed ceiling extends over two floors high. On both sides of this are courtyards around which rooms are organised, a stairway that leads to the upstairs deck, where you can lean on the balustrade and gaze down into the hall.

Built in 1922, by R.M.P.R.M.M Subramanya Chettiar (aka Chinna Subbaiyar Chettiar), Valliappa's paternal grandfather, the fifty-room house is spread over two floors, with Burma teak used liberally. The main pillars are made of granite.

The Sona Story

Photographs of the house in its heyday are lovingly preserved, and Valliappa points with pride to one particular image of the spectacular facade of the home. A deer is peeping over the wall, a horse is standing in front of the door as is a dashing vintage convertible with a uniformed driver. 'He had bulls, cows, horses and deer and was the first to get an imported car,' says Valliappa of his flamboyant grandfather.

'He was also a really bold and fearless person,' says Valliappa. 'Once he was taking rest in the veranda, with an attendant sitting nearby keeping watch. Suddenly the attendant spotted a big snake slithering nearby. Though petrified, the attendant did not want to disturb his master. He swooped down and caught the snake with his hands, holding it behind its head and its tail. At that moment Ayyah woke up and saw the scene. But he had such presence of mind that he quickly took out his penknife and slashed the snake into two,' says Valliappa.

Subramanya Chettiar enjoyed the good things in life and spent lavishly. The people of Poolankurichi called him Ottuvettukarar as he was the first to build an ottuvedu (tiled-roof house) in the village. He was also the first in the village to own a car, a Chevrolet. But he loved to travel in a bullock cart – the common means of transport between villages those days. Valliappa says long journeys on the bullock carts were akin to the stage coach journeys in Britain, where after every six hours or so the tired horses would be changed for healthy, rested ones. Similarly, the bullocks would be changed.

Chuckling, Valliappa recounts how people and their homes got names. A house with huge plantains in the garden was called Valamarathu Kaar Veedu (the home of the people with the plantains). Another was called Aeroplane Kaar Veedu (the house of the pilot). The funniest, he says, was a house called Idli Azhagi Veedu (the beautiful idli home). The story goes that the newly married girl who arrived here was tasked with making idlis early in the morning. She kept pouring the batter into the moulds without lining them with white muslin. In those days the moulds had big holes; therefore, the wet cloth was important to prevent the batter from dripping down. Instead of being steamed, the batter seeped through the holes. And the people in that house never lived it down.

Valliappa says Subramanya Chettiar's income fluctuated greatly. He tended to spend more than he earned. But he was known for his mediation skills and was called to resolve numerous jurisdictional issues. Notably, he was pressed upon to resolve a dispute in Pillayarpatti where a few people had taken control of the famous temple, for which Subramanya Chettiar formed the Pillayarpatti Karpaga Vinayagar Nagarathar Trust.

The Chettiar lifestyle was a quaint amalgam of very traditional, local customs and global ones absorbed from their travels abroad. In the olden days, when the Chettiars were stationed in Colombo, Malaysia and Burma, a notable feature at many of their homes was the huge money chests – almost as large as a cot – where the daily collections were kept. As an additional safety measure, the munim, or accountant, would sleep on top of the box at night. 'The place that the Chettiars used as both office and a place to rest, especially in Singapore, was called kittangi, a sort of warehouse,' explains Valliappa.

The name of the village Poolankurichi, which means in and around mountains, Valliappa says, came from the hillocks in the distance. In the old days, those hillocks served as hiding places for the locals to repel British attacks.

Although Valliappa only spent holidays at Poolankurichi, he has fond memories of playing with cousins in the ancestral home. Etched on the floors of the veranda upstairs, leading to the colonnaded balcony, is the ancient boardgame Thayam – a dice game similar to Ludo – that they played there. Boardgames and storytelling, especially tales from the epics narrated by elderly aunts and uncles, were the chief entertainment of the time. Valliappa remembers the fragrance of flowers, Irrutu kadai halwa (halwa from the famous shop in Tirunelveli) and colourful festivals at Poolankurichi.

Back in the day, kitchens and toilets were typically placed at the back of the house in different units separated from the main home by a garden. During restoration of the house, Valliappa broached the subject with architect Vikram Ponappa – should they introduce modern conveniences inside the home or not. Finally, a concession to modernity was made but in a way that it blends into the traditional architecture.

The cuisine of Chettinad is very distinctive – the use of aromatic spices, sun-dried meats and salted vegetables, and rich gravies reflects the dry climate of the region. The Chettiars were traditionally vegetarian but their travels all over for trade influenced what they ate and gave birth to a fusion cuisine called Chettinad, which has earned fame for the complexity of its flavours and heat of its meaty curries. Rice-based dishes are the staple, served up in myriad ways.

The Valliappas are, unlike most of their community, staunchly vegetarian, thanks to the influence of their maternal grandfather, 'Textile King' Karumuttu Thiagarajar Chettiar, who had a close connection with Mahatma Gandhi.

Blessed by Bapu

It was at Karumuttu Thiagarajar Chettiar's house in West Masi Road in Madurai that Gandhiji took the vow to adopt the loincloth as his attire in 1921. The reason for the change is well known – he had been advocating the use of indigenously spun and produced khadi to liberate India from colonial rule.

However, during his journey to Madurai by train he understood that for common folk any sort of clothes was a luxury as the poorest could not afford it. Karumuttu Thiagarajar's wife, Radha, penned a biography of her husband, in which she says: 'Gandhi's momentous decision was taken when he was in Kalaithanthi's house. Kalaithanthi has mentioned this in a letter to Rajaji. Even now there is a board at the front of the house mentioning that Gandhi took to loincloth when he had been staying in that house.'[5]

Says Valliappa, 'He went into my grandfather's home as Mohandas Karamchand Gandhi and came out as Mahatma Gandhi.'

Radha Thiagarajan says in the book that it was the Gujarati businessman Kalyanji Ramji who prevailed upon Gandhiji to stay as Kalaithanthi's guest.

The friendship between Karumuttu Thiagarajar Chettiar and Gandhiji began when an impassioned piece the former wrote about an injustice he witnessed in Sri Lanka caught the eyes of the Mahatma, who was at that time fighting for the rights of workers in mines in South Africa.

Thiagarajar Chettiar had been asked by the UK Commission to write a report on the state of tea garden workers in Sri Lanka. When he went there, he was deeply disturbed to see a tea garden worker shot in the leg by her supervisor for reporting sick, and he poured out his angst about the plight of the downtrodden workers in a piece in the newspaper *Morning Leader*. This led to correspondence between Gandhiji and Thiagarajar Chettiar and a bond was forged. Incidentally, both Gandhiji and Thiagarajar Chettiar returned to their homeland in the same year – 1916.

Gandhiji's views on education were that it was necessary for socio-economic development, for the attainment of peace and for personality development. He believed vocational training or some scheme of education which provides work experience was most important. He wanted Indians to become self-reliant.

Deeply influenced by his views, Thiagarajar Chettiar took over a textile mill in Salem that had laid off hundreds of workers. He realised he needed to train the workers and set about creating educational institutions that would impart practical skills.

He developed many textile mills to promote and develop the Indian weaving framework. He was inspired by the Tamil language, passionate about Indian music and excelled at engineering. He earned the sobriquet Kalaithanthi for his patronage of arts. His administrative and business abilities were legendary, and everything he touched flourished. He was a great lover of buildings and architecture, and all his buildings carried a distinctive stamp.

Over the years, his son-in-law M.S. Chockalingam Chettiar and his grandson Valliappa carried forward Karumuttu's legacy, expanding and scaling up the educational institutions in Salem.

An Inheritance of Values

Valliappa's father, Chockalingam Chettiar, was born at the ancestral house in Poolankurichi. At the age of twelve, he was sent to Madurai Sethupathi School, where the poet and social reformer Subramania Bharati worked. He graduated from the American College, one of the oldest colleges in India, set up in 1891 by American missionaries.

His wife, Meenakshi, daughter of Karumuttu Thiagarajar, was educated in Madurai. Karumuttu Thiagarajar had a profound influence on the Valliappas and shaped their business philosophy and ideals of empowerment. From him they imbibed the values of treating workers well and empowering women.

That Chockalingam and Meenakshi would get married was decided when they were young children. But Karumuttu frowned upon child marriage and was clear that his daughter would not get married before the age of eighteen. He took Chockalingam, then aged twelve, under his wing and took him to Madurai to be educated. A very close bond developed between the two.

Young Chockalingam was an extrovert and fun-loving. He liked to shimmy up coconut trees and ask his mother-in-law-to-be if he could pluck coconuts for her. 'Look what you did, you got such a boisterous boy and we have to take care of him now,' she would joke with her husband.

The Origins

The Karumuttu family traces its origins to Karungulam, a small village on the outskirts of Pattamangalam in old Ramanathapuram district. From there they moved to Athikkadu Thekkur. Thiagarajar's paternal grandfather was Karuppan Chettiar and his son Muthukaruppan Chettiar was Thiagarajar's father. The family name Karumuttu is a portmanteau of these names.

Muthukaruppan Chettiar was a highly progressive man, and the first to break from tradition and get out of the community business of moneylending. He entered the textile trade, importing fabric from England and selling it in Sri Lanka and India. In the good old days, there used to be a Karumuttu house in Colombo. A staunch vegetarian, Muthukaruppan infused vegetarianism in his family. He believed in doing projects that would benefit the community and laid the road from Athikkadu Thekkur to Thirupathur. He was full of reformist zeal, which he passed on to his children.

Muthukaruppan had ten children – four sons and six daughters. Karumuthu Thiagarajar was the youngest.

Muthukaruppan's second son, Alagappa Chettiar, fought hard to stop animal sacrifice in temples, and he also campaigned to change the dress code of Chettiar women that forbade them from wearing a blouse or top.

But it was the Colombo-educated Karumuttu Thiagarajar who achieved huge business success. He set up fourteen textile mills, the biggest of which was Sri Meenakshi Mills. Most of his ventures were successful, but had their ups and downs.

Valliappa recounts how when Karumuttu returned from Colombo, he had an urge to start a business. The dominant textile mills of that time were run by the British – Binnys (Buckingham Mill in Madras), Harveys (A&F Harvey Mills in Madurai which later became Madura Coats) and Stanes (Coimbatore Spinning and Weaving Mills). But Harvey Mills in Madurai faced labour problems and strikes and many workers lost their jobs. The retrenched workers approached several Indian businessmen to start a mill. Eventually, the Gujarati businessman Kalyanji Ramji, who ran Kalyani Mills in Madras, agreed to start a unit in Madurai, on the condition that Karumuttu, who was actively championing the workers, would join as director. That was how Meenakshi Mills was born. But even before the mill could begin production, it had piled on huge debts and Kalyanji wanted out – he appealed to Karumuttu to take over the company.

Karumuttu also set up the Bank of Madura and Madurai Insurance Company. More important, he set up nineteen educational institutes, among them the Thiagarajar Polytechnic College (TPT) in Salem, which his son-in-law Chockalingam Chettiar built and managed.

Chockalingam Chettiar soon became a favourite of the Karumuttu family, and later, when a dispute arose among the children of the Thiagarajar family, he was drawn in to resolve it. Karumuttu would often consult his son-in-law on many issues, including buying land, cars and cows.

The Nagarathar Way: The Chettiar Heritage

Like his father, Chinna Subbaiyar Chettiar, Chockalingam was proficient at resolving disputes. But unlike his father who was a bit of a spendthrift, Chockalingam was frugal and careful and managed to stabilise the family fortunes.

Valliappa remembers how his father used to start his day with a brisk round of walking, followed by meditation and several yoga asanas, including sirsasana, for a number of years. When he turned seventy-five, doctors dissuaded him from practising sirsasana, though Valliappa feels that that was the secret to his good health. He recounts that his father had a special interest in horticulture and cattle breeding and groomed the cattle every day. He was pious and interested in music and travelling.

Since Chockalingam was vested with the care of the Sree Rajendra Mills by Karumuttu, he shifted to Salem and ran it with great passion, and under his watch the Thiagarajar Polytechnic College, which he had begun to manage, grew in stature.

The campus became his passion, and when he was eighty-six, he established the Sona College of Technology, Salem along with Valliappa in 1997. His extraordinary zeal earned him the title 'Saleathu Semmal' or forceful personality. Interestingly, the Sona Group got its name from the nickname that Chockalingam's friends and admirers gave him.

Karumuttu also entrusted the mills he had acquired in Salem to Chockalingam. In a fascinating coincidence, the two mills in Salem, established pre-Independence, were called Rajendra Mills and Jawahar Mills. 'Perhaps the founder was prescient that they would be the names of the first president and first prime minister of India,' says Valliappa with a chuckle. It was in Rajendra Mills that Valliappa cut his teeth in the textiles business.

Growing up, Valliappa was greatly influenced by both his father and his mother. His mother, Karumuttu's daughter Meenakshi Aachi, was ahead of her times in the way she batted for women's empowerment. 'She was a tall lady, nearly five feet seven inches, and her posture was always ramrod straight. This made her look taller,' says Valliappa. Both Chockalingam and Meenakshi Aachi were considerate towards the workers and supported their betterment. With her progressive ideas, she embodied what the poet Subramania Bharati referred to as Pudhumai Penn (modern Indian woman). From her father she inherited her love for Tamil literature and music. Karumuttu had insisted that all his daughters should learn music and got M.S. Subbalakshmi's mother, Shanmuga Vadivu, who resided in Madurai, to teach them to play the harmonium.

Meenakshi Aachi was a talented homemaker who made her house a real home. 'She was also a very strict lady, though affectionate, and even at the age of eighty, she stood upright,' says Valliappa. Chocko remembers fondly how she used to pace up and down the veranda for hours waiting to greet her children and grandchildren when they were expected from Bengaluru.

Chockalingam and Meenakshi were blessed with six children – Sundaram, Thyagaraja, Saraswathi, Dhanalakshmi, Kamala and Valliappa. A really cute-looking baby, Valliappa, born on 19 July 1943, the youngest in the family, was the apple of everyone's eyes. He recalls how his mother, Meenakshi Aachi, would never let him outside, and if he went out, she would carry out rituals to ward off the evil eye. While their childhood was harmonious, in later years, to Valliappa's great sadness, his eldest brother and he had a discordant relationship, marred by property disputes.

Just a year before Valliappa was born, the entire nation was rocked by the Quit India Movement. The 1942 movement impacted Madurai city too, where Chockalingam Chettiar and Meenakshi Aachi lived before they moved to Salem. In August 1942, a European couple was stoned in Madurai. Workers at Madurai Mills went on agitation. Frequent clashes took place between the freedom fighters and the British administration.

The Nagarathar Way: The Chettiar Heritage

Telegraph posts were sabotaged in Usilampatti, and the city remained tense.

Discussions at home revolved a lot around the freedom struggles, and the call for swadeshi touched them. However, despite the undercurrents, life went on normally and did not affect the children much.

Growing up in Madurai, Valliappa's fondest memories are of the Madurai Meenakshi Amman festival, a most awaited event for the kids. While the adults would fast and visit the temple for the evening aarati and also to catch a glimpse of the most powerful goddesses, the children indulged in their favourite pastime – wheeling old bicycle tyres with little sticks. Finally after days of fasting, praying and evening aaratis, the goddesses in all their glory would be carried on a palanquin towards the lake in a grand procession People would celebrate the arrival of their beloved goddesses and with this the festivities would wind down only to come back after one year when the goddesses returned to their people. 'It was very crowded,' remembers Valliappa.

During the school vacations, the Chockalingam family would go to Kodaikanal or to Courtallam, where Karumuttu had built many palatial homes. 'Every year from the first of April to the thirty-first of May, grandfather would be in Kodaikanal. When he went, he would transfer practically the whole household, even taking his cows with him,' recalls Valliappa. 'We would spend two months there.' From 1 June to 15 August, Karumuttu would move his entourage to Courtallam, where he had magnificent residences. Here he would hold a sabha (gathering) of an eclectic mix of writers, poets, politicians and industrialists, akin to a mini Davos of modern times.

Although Valliappa lived only for five to six years in Madurai, the city is close to his heart and the connection lingers. 'It is like a living, breathing organism,' he says. He says the people of

Madurai have the inexplicable ability to make one feel warm and loved even if one is a complete stranger and it is something he hasn't experienced to this degree in other places he visited around India.

For Valliappa, his father was a revered figure and quite a role model. He speaks of his tolerance, patience, belief in God and hard work — values that he has tried to imbibe. As Valliappa was the youngest son in the family and the youngest boy among all cousins from his father's side, he was pampered a lot in his childhood. In the 1950s, he studied in Bharathi Vidhyalaya in Madurai up to the seventh standard and then went to Little Flower, a famous school in Salem.

He was very close to his middle brother, Thyagaraja, who died early of cancer. Believing that the cancer was cured, the family had fixed Thyagaraja's marriage. But he did not get a chance to meet the girl, and no amount of pleading with his parents did any good. Thyagaraja appealed to Valliappa, who was then in his late teens, to plead his case. 'My parents were ignoring my requests too, so I just took the car and drove off to Karaikudi in a huff. In two days, I was traced and my parents said my brother could go meet his chosen bride,' says Valliappa with a grin. Even at a young age, he was adept at getting his way.

3

The Young Student Leader

THE AMERICAN AUTHOR Robert Greene once wrote, 'Your college education is a key moment in life.' For Valliappa college education was surely a defining moment in his life, as it was here that his leadership qualities burst to the fore.

But we are getting ahead of the story. Like in most families, a lot of thought was given to which college and stream Valliappa should choose. But ultimately, his parents left the choice entirely to him. Loyola College in Chennai was considered the best college in Tamil Nadu at the time. Initially, he enrolled at Loyola College. But after a month of deliberation Valliappa decided to study commerce in Pachaiyappa's College. He graduated in 1964.

An influencing factor in Valliappa's choice was that Pachaiyappa's, founded in 1842, was the first educational institution in south India not funded by the British. Its Indo-Saracenic architecture was grand, and it had a redoubtable list of alumni ranging from fiery politician C.N. Annadurai to Vijayrangam Sambandam Mudaliar, the doyen of Tamil theatre. With a mischievous grin Valliappa says another important factor that swayed his selection of college was that he wanted to have more fun and freedom to do things he was passionate about. Loyola was known to be regimented, while Pachaiyappa's was more relaxed and had a lot of extracurricular activities.

In college, Valliappa came into his own. He was fully involved in students' welfare associations. Encouraged by his friends, he contended for the post of chairman of the commerce association. But he was not elected. It was a jolt. However, he knew that things would eventually fall into place, and sure enough, within a week, he was nominated for the position of student president of the college union. In a surprising twist of fate, the same student who was not elected for the post of chairman of the commerce association was elected as the students' chairman of the entire college.

As Valliappa relates the incident, he quotes a Thiruvasagam hymn (written by the Bhakti poet Mannikavasagar):

வேண்டத் தக்கது அறிவோய் நீ!
வேண்ட முழுதும் தருவோய் நீ!
வேண்டும் அயன், மாற்கு, அரியாய் நீ!
வேண்டி, என்னைப் பணி கொண்டாய்;
வேண்டி நீ யாது அருள் செய்தாய்,
யானும், அதுவே வேண்டின் அல்லால்,
வேண்டும், பரிசு ஒன்று உண்டென்னில்,
அதுவும், உன் தன் விருப்பன்றே?
-குழைத்தபத்து, திருவாசகம்

You know what to pray for!
When prayed, you answer all those prayers!
You are the God worshiped even by Brahma and Vishnu,
we worship!
As prayed, you took over me!
For praying, what have you destined me to,
If I too don't pray for the same destined prayer,
But I am in search of a different gift,
Isn't that too as per your wish?!
[Kuzhaithapathu 6 – Thiruvasagam]

The Young Student Leader

Through this incident, Valliappa says, he understood that God works in strange ways – he may not grant you what you wish for at once, but may outdo it later, with a better thing. As the students' chairman, Valliappa flung himself into his duties assiduously under the guidance of their principal, C.D. Rajeswaran. Slowly he gained confidence and began to command the admiration of his peers, who began to look at him for guidance. Several people approached him with their problems and it was interesting, he says, to apply his mind to solve those. Many of these were minor hostel issues that were easily resolved amicably.

For instance, once a fight erupted between two of his hostel mates, each vying for their own space in their room. Valliappa intervened and drew a line down the middle of the room for the two friends to find their own space. In that simple act of delineation, Valliappa transformed what could have been a battlefield into a playground of harmony. His good-natured approach to conflict resolution was not merely about dividing space, it was about bridging hearts. With a touch of humour and a dash of diplomacy, he turned adversaries into allies, laying the foundation for enduring friendships. His ability to empathise and find common ground in the most unlikely of places became the cornerstone of his character.

As a college union leader, Valliappa met many tall leaders of the time such as Periyar, Kamarajar and Annadurai. In connection with university programmes, he met Karmaveerar Kamarajar, the then chief minister of Madras, on three memorable occasions. Kamarajar was known as the kingmaker of the Indian National Congress, and had refused to become prime minister even though the post was offered to him, instead elevating Lal Bahadur Shastri and later Indira Gandhi. Following the India–China war Valliappa collected ₹1719 for the Prime Minister's Relief Fund and handed it over to Kamaraj.

The Sona Story

Equally memorable was the meeting with Annadurai, who later became the chief minister. He was the last chief minister of Madras State, which was renamed Tamil Nadu in January 1969. Annadurai also became the first chief minister of the newly named state.

Valliappa remembers the day Anna, as Annadurai was called, visited the college. The college auditorium was packed well in advance and a hum of anticipation permeated the crowd. Anna was hugely popular and known for his witty oratorical style. Seeing the noisy auditorium, Valliappa took Annadurai safely to the stage through the rear gate, bypassing the crowd. When Annadurai reached the stage, the crowd was surprised. As he started his address, the first thing the leader humorously said was how he felt his entrance to the college was similar to entering Parliament – through the back door. It was a reference to the 1962 elections when Dravida Munnetra Kazhagam (DMK) had become a big political power in the state, winning fifty assembly seats, but Anna had lost the election as a member of the Legislative Assembly from Kanchipuram constituency. He was later nominated to the Rajya Sabha and became a member of Parliament. The audience was charmed by his ability to joke at himself. He said he felt honoured at being given 'a Z+ level protection' by the college, crediting Valliappa for whisking him in without encountering crowds. In the same meeting, Anna said: 'If you are a friend, give me suggestions; if you are a foe, I will ignore you.' These words struck a chord with Valliappa and he let them guide his actions ever since.

During his college days, Valliappa met various prominent political figures. A particularly memorable encounter was with the second president of India, Dr S. Radhakrishnan, during his visit to Pachaiyappa's College on 5 January 1963, when he unveiled the life-sized statue of Pachaiyappa Mudaliar, the college's founder. For Valliappa, who as student chairman, had the duty of escorting the president of India to the statue, it was an amazing opportunity to engage with the scholarly leader.

Apart from leaders and statesmen, Valliappa also had lovely interactions with cultural icons like lyricist Kannadasan and Carnatic music legend M.S. Subbulakshmi. As the head of the Nagarathar Students' Association, he met Kannadasan and received a donation of ₹300, a princely sum those days, for the welfare of the association.

When Valliappa had the privilege of meeting C. Rajagopalachari, fondly called Rajaji, at journalist, film producer and freedom fighter Kalki Sadasivam's home, it led to a remarkable encounter with a singer he had long admired – M.S. Subbulakshmi, who was married to Sadasivam. Rajaji and Sadasivam were residing in adjacent buildings, setting the stage for Valliappa's memorable interaction with not one but three luminaries. During their initial meeting, a special connection formed between Valliappa and Subbulakshmi. She exhibited genuine warmth and concern, even making a thoughtful observation about Valliappa's acne skin condition, suggesting a traditional solution with punugu (organic skincare) paste. Living as I do in a hostel, where can I get punugu? Valliappa asked her. MS asked him not to worry and that she would arrange it for him. 'It was unbelievable that a celebrity like MS would take the trouble and collect punugu for me,' he recalls. Valliappa reflects on this gesture with surprised gratitude, marvelling at MS's unexpected kindness.

During his college years, Valliappa consistently exhibited leadership qualities. An incident that highlighted this involved Kumari Sachu, a Tamil actress, who once had graced the college's cultural programme. Unruly behaviour from students marred her performance, with students disrupting the event by creating paper planes to pelt at her. The students' behaviour was beyond the control of faculty members and the college principal.

Despite not holding an official leadership position among the students, Valliappa found himself with the responsibility of restoring order at the behest of the new principal. Respecting the principal's directive, Valliappa swiftly took charge of the situation, leveraging his innate leadership skills to quell the unruliness and ensure decorum was restored.

Throughout his term as students' chairman, Valliappa consistently demonstrated strong leadership in various situations. He himself considers his most significant achievements to be the maintenance of peace and harmony within Pachaiyappa's College, as his tenure witnessed no student unrest.

Valliappa's deep passion for Tamil and English literature, instilled by his father Chockalingam Chettiar, prompted him to initiate events that celebrated language and culture. One notable initiative was his invitation to S.A.P. Annamalai, the founder of *Kumudam* magazine, to speak at the Nagarathar Sangam in his college. Annamalai was reluctant, but Valliappa, with his characteristic persuasive skills, convinced Annamalai to grace the college with his presence. The event orchestrated by Valliappa unfolded seamlessly and earned him accolades for his organisational skills.

Afterwards, Valliappa had a long chat with Annamalai regarding his reticence towards public speaking despite his eloquent writing and strong communication skills. Annamalai candidly shared his perspective, emphasising the necessity of prioritising his responsibilities at *Kumudam* over frequent public engagements. It was a conversation from which Valliappa took away a valuable lesson – the importance of unwavering focus and dedication towards achieving one's goals. Annamalai's single-minded commitment to his role at *Kumudam* impressed young Valliappa, and in later years when he had to jostle between public engagements and business tasks, this incident would often remind him where his priorities lay.

The Young Student Leader

There were other lessons he learned from the people he encountered during his college days. In those days, all the colleges were affiliated with Madras University, where A.L. Mudaliar served as the vice-chancellor. Valliappa's decision to invite Mudaliar to a college event was driven by not only self-interest but also by a genuine desire to foster connections and enrich the college community. He went for the meeting wearing a formal western suit and looking dapper, assuming the vice-chancellor would be well dressed. However, upon arriving at Mudhaliyar's office, Valliappa encountered a person dressed in exceedingly plain and unassuming clothes. Initially surprised, Valliappa was impressed by the simplicity of the man. This incident taught Valliappa that appearances can be deceptive and that one had to look beyond the surface.

Valliappa's college journey was enriched by meaningful connections with influential figures who would later rise to prominent positions in academia. One such person was M. Varatharajanar, known as Mu.Va., who had a close and lasting bond with Valliappa. As destiny would have it, Varatharajanar went on to become vice-chancellor at Madurai Kamaraj University. Valliappa also shared a deep bond with C. Balasubramaniam, a connection that would prove to be invaluable in the years to come. Balasubramaniam's journey led him to the position of vice-chancellor at Tamil University in 1989, where his dedication to education and scholarly pursuits would leave a lasting impact. When Valliappa was spearheading the Sona Group of educational institutions, these college connections came in helpful as he could simply reach out to them for guidance.

Valliappa's college days were characterised by a remarkable display of self-discipline. Despite the temptations and distractions that often accompany hostel life, Valliappa refused to be swayed, and remained focused on his goals.

Valliappa was also profoundly influenced by Rajaji, whose public speeches he heard on radio and live, especially those delivered in his college. He recalls one particular line of Rajaji, 'A government without opposition is a vehicle without tyre.' This made him welcome criticism.

The college years also cemented some beautiful friendships. S.S. Meenakshi Sundaram and Selvaganapathi, who were his hostel mates, became good friends. Recalling those years, Meenakshi Sundaram, fondly called So So Me, who was doing his MCom degree in Pachaiyappa's College while Valliappa was doing his BCom, says how Valliappa was always concerned about the students' community. Valliappa was an active participant in the youth wing of the Nagarathar Association. He recalled how he got his grandfather Karumuttu Chettiar to give a special talk at the Nagarathar Association, and the great love and respect they had for each other.

Sundaram says that what struck him at the time was Valliappa's ability to be on the same wavelength with anyone he met, regardless of age. 'That's a rare quality,' he says. Even at age eighty years, Valliappa is the same, avers Sundaram, pointing out how he still maintains the same rapport with people, and can converse with ease with everyone.

Sundaram reminisces that Valliappa was a quick learner and had a retentive memory. He had the knack of pulling out information from the recesses of his mind when ideating on something new. He also lauded the busy industrialist for being a true and loyal friend and said that 'shared beliefs and experiences' united them. Above all, he admires Valliappa's indefatigable energy as he travels from Salem to Bengaluru, and then to Madurai or Poolankurichi, without showing any tiredness.

Many teachers became friends and mentors to Valliappa. Among them, Satya Moorthy, a senior auditor, played a pivotal role, imparting invaluable lessons in accountancy and auditing. Their bond extended beyond the classroom, with Satya Moorthy often joining Valliappa for lunch in his room, fostering a mentorship that went beyond the confines of formal education. Valliappa's favourite teachers were Prof. Venkat Rao, Johnson, Nacky Chidambaram, Ranganathan (Economics), Kowsi and Vadivel (Commerce).

In college Valliappa chose to study Hindi as his second language despite his passion for Tamil, driven by a desire to expand his horizons. In Tamil Nadu, which had seen moves to resist imposition of Hindi, and language was an emotive issue, this was a big step, exemplifying Valliappa's willingness to embrace diverse perspectives.

Interestingly, his grandfather had had differences with Rajaji in 1937 over Hindi. In that year, Rajaji had become the prime minister of Madras state, and with Congress passsing a resolution that Hindi should be official language in free India, Rajaji made it a compulsory language to be taught in schools in Tamil Nadu. Karumuttu, Valliappa's grandfather, was deeply concerned the move would affect Tamil and wrote to Rajaji saying Hindi should be gradually introduced as an optional language in colleges rather than being imposed. Later in 1965, in free India, when there was talk of Hindi being selected as the sole official language, anti-Hindi feelings ran high in Tamil Nadu. So it was all the more interesting that Valliappa chose to follow his own conviction on the matter of Hindi.

For Valliappa, college life was a brilliant journey with spring in each step, fervour in mind and a lilt in the heart.

Years later, stories of his college days inspired his sons, Chocko and Thyagu, to emulate him and join student union activities. Chocko became the president of the student union during his time at Christ College, Bengaluru. 'Looking at the pictures of my father with Radhakrishnan and Kamarajar, a spark was lit in me and I also plunged into union activities,' says Chocko.

In the first year, he contested for the post of union secretary and won by a sweeping margin. 'I came home and got an entire lesson on being a union leader from my father. He said to me being a leader is to lead the students in the right way and not mislead them. Organising a strike is easy. Getting what you want is the basic objective, focus on the outcome. Make Christ College a better college.'

A year later, in 1987, Chocko became the union chairman and worked to make the college a better institution. It was the first year that Christ College did not have a strike, he says. Says Valliappa, 'Today, Christ has attained the status of a prestigious university – a fine one at that. Perhaps my words were prophetic.'

In the family tradition, Thyagu too participated wholeheartedly in Christ College union activities making significant contributions. Perhaps the union stints contributed to the empathetic leadership style of the Valliappas.

4

Valliappa, the Family Man

A FAMILY IS SAID to be the first school of a child. It is here one starts to learn to speak, walk and interact with the world. Our family builds our character and fortunate are those who have the love and support of their family. Valliappa acknowledges the immense role his family has played in his success, saying, 'Family has been my backbone.'

Finding a Soulmate

The Nagarathar community is traditional when it comes to marriages – following the age-old practice of matching horoscopes to determine the compatibility of the bride and the groom. The wedding ceremony is lavish and spread over many days.

As was the norm, Valliappa's match was arranged by his family. As he points out, 'A wedding is treated as a very important event in the Nagarathar community. Historically it used to take place over thirteen to fifteen days. My father's stretched over thirteen days. Mine was elaborate too, but it happened over just four days. Nowadays it has been condensed to just one or two days as was the case with my sons.'

The pre-wedding ceremonies include nischaythartham (consent) and peshimudithal (agreement) – one at the bride's home and one at the groom's home – with a generous exchange of gifts. 'In our family, we do not have too many of these,' stresses Valliappa.

Typically, as the first step, the groom goes to the bride's house to ask for her hand, and thus with mutual understanding of both the families, a date is fixed for the wedding. There are some quaint rituals like the mulaiparikattdal, where seven types of grains soaked in milk and water are put in five different pots. Once they sprout they are tied to a lengthy pole. This symbolises the happy and healthy blooming life of the couple.

Another ritual is Kottai kattudal, which originated over four hundred years ago when kings and queens ruled over the land and were the chief patrons of all big events. The Nagarathar community used to construct a structure out of grains and gift it to the king and convey the information about a new groom in the family. Over time as the feudal system fell away, the ritual evolved. The community now ties up all the grains and makes a groom cross over it, announcing him as the bride's chosen groom.

There are some fun rituals like pen edikkikaatudhal (lifting the bride) on the wedding day. The ritual started when child marriages were prevalent. Marriages were solemnised when a boy was barely ten and the girl was seven or eight. Hence during the rituals, the child bride would be carried by her family for the groom to view. Now even though child marriage has been abolished, the practice of pen edikkikaatudhal continues and contributes to much merriment.

Seetha Achi shares another ritual harking back to feudal times: arasaani kaal kattudhal. In those days, the king was the royal guest at weddings. But now, precious stones are used in lieu of the royal guest. Pavizham (coral), arasa ilai (sacred fig leaf), maav ilai (mango leaves), kiluvey (frankincense) are powdered and mixed in an arasaani (a kind of stone every

Nagarathar community house has) and this is tied to a pole symbolising the royal presence of the king in the rituals.

Another ritual is that of Thiruputrasadangu (seven small beakers on a plate). An idol of Lord Ganesha is placed in the centre of the plate and beakers filled with kumkum, chandan, thiruneer, rice, salt, tamarind and betel leaf are placed around the idol. The mother-in-law of the family should use the items on the plate first and then the daughter-in-law. The significance of this ritual being that all the properties which belong to the mother-in-law will belong to the daughter-in-law. Not just the ornaments, but also the salt and tamarind.

Then there is the Poomanaiduthal (jasmine and milk ritual). The newly married couple are blessed with jasmine and milk. Changes are inevitable as times evolve, but even now most of these elaborate rituals are followed, says Seetha Aachi.

Valliappa's wedding followed the fairy-tale traditions of yore and were packed with many of these rituals. He got married at the age of twenty-two. Valliappa's one and only expectation of his betrothed was that she should be a graduate. His parents adhered to his wish and the family selected Seetha Aachi, who had a home science degree to her credit. It was his grandfather who chose his bride, who was distantly related to the family.

Seetha Aachi's father was in banking, financing and film distribution, spending a considerable part of his career in Colombo. The children studied in Madurai but often visited him in Sri Lanka. Seetha Aachi was fairly cosmopolitan having travelled a lot and even watched films being shot as her father financed several movies. One notable film that he backed was the first production of superstar M.G. Ramachandran, better known as MGR, *Nadudi Mannan*, which became a massive hit. Seetha Aachi recalls, 'MGR was nervous about the film's reception. He told my father, "If the film flops, I will be a nadudi [a common man], and if it succeeds, I will be no less than a mannan [king].'" Much to everyone's relief the film was a major hit and made MGR a superhero.

Seetha Aachi recalls that when the film became a great hit, her father went to the superstar and offered him a silver pot. It was a Friday. MGR hesitated. Then he told her father, 'I would love to accept this token. But it is not considered good for the giver to give a pot on Friday. For your sake I am requesting you to come and give me this on another day.'

Valliappa speaks with pride about his in-laws. His wife has five brothers and three sisters. 'Seetha's brother is a dedicated doctor. He did his master's in medicine from UK and worked in Boulton Hospital in Manchester. The amazing thing about him is he retired from there having worked forty years without taking a single day's sick leave. In appreciation, the government has given him a special pension,' he says.

Though born into a rich family, Seetha Aachi was well versed in household chores. Valliappa recalls that when his chithi and chithappa (maternal aunt and uncle) went to meet his betrothed for the first time, they found her cooking in the home science college kitchen, wearing a white apron and white cap.

Says Valliappa, 'The marriage was considered pretty unusual as both the bride and groom were graduates – a rarity those days!'

The betrothal took place in Madurai, and Valliappa and Seetha Aachi were married on 27 January 1966 with the blessings of Valliappa's paternal and maternal grandfathers at Kandavarayanpatti, the bride's ancestral village, in Chettinad.

Valliappa says his wife has been the invisible force holding the family together with warmth, understanding and affection. Seetha Aachi joined the Salem household and fit in beautifully. She says her mother-in-law was very kind.

Valliappa, the Family Man

A year into their marriage, in January 1967, Valliappa moved to Bengaluru to oversee the construction of a mill his father was building on the outskirts of the city in Ramanagara. 'I migrated to Bengaluru in January. The mill was inaugurated on 20 April 1967. Seetha Aachi shifted a few months later as Chocko was a six-month-old baby at the time.' They settled down in a rented four-bedroom house in Lavelle Road.

Two momentous events happened in Valliappa's life – the birth of a son and the birth of the mill. Those were days of hard work as Valliappa threw himself into learning every aspect of the mill's operations. Business often kept Valliappa away from home for long stretches, but Seetha Aachi never complained. She managed the family alone at those times with great skill. Visitors were constant – with many comings and goings of family from Salem and Madurai. Valliappa speaks with deep appreciation of her hospitality and how she treated all her guests royally. During those days, Seetha Aachi was a pillar of support, he says. Although fully immersed in his work, Valliappa would find time for all the important family events, ensuring he was present.

Valliappa and Seetha were blessed with two sons, and as is the Nagarathar tradition they were named after their grandparents. Chocko Valliappa, the elder son, was named after Chockalingam Chettiar, and Thyagu Valliappa, the younger one, got his name from his maternal grandfather as well as great-grandfather Thiagarajar Chettiar.

Chocko was born prematurely in late 1966 while Thyagu was born in the winter of 1972. As was the custom, Seetha Aachi went to her maternal home for delivery and both boys were delivered by Dr Grace Kennet, Madurai's best-known gynaecologist since pre-Independence days and a redoubtable lady. Interestingly, the same doctor had delivered Valliappa, Seetha Aachi and her mother too. Always dressed in white,

The Sona Story

Dr Kennet worked with the American Mission Hospital, before founding her own maternity hospital in Madurai.

Seetha Aachi recalls, 'I was ill throughout my first pregnancy, and when I went for delivery to my parents' home in Madurai, the doctors wanted to get me admitted at once. But my father decided to take a second opinion and that's how we met Dr Grace, who reassured us and told us there was no need to be admitted.'

Valliappa and his sons have always had an easy-going relationship, talking and communicating a lot. Not an action is taken without the sons being informed on the phone. Even when they were small children, Valliappa would take them along with him to the factory or to the bank. It was an interesting time for the boys as they subconsciously absorbed a lot of things about running a business.

Thyagu recalls how he would visit the mill and play cricket with the workers. On occasion, a visiting MLA would join in too. H.D. Kumaraswamy and Basavaraj Bommai, both of whom later went on to become chief ministers of Karnataka, were frequent visitors. Those were carefree days without much formality, when politicians mingled freely.

Valliappa has a wealth of stories about his two sons. He chuckles when he recounts how on a Sunday, when a set of overseas visitors were arriving, he sent five-year-old Chocko with the driver to the airport to receive them. When the visitors, who were large built men, arrived, they were surprised to see a small boy come up to them and tell them he had been sent to meet them.

One memorable incident the family still chuckles over when they gather for their meals is of the time Chocko accompanied his dad to the bank. He was about eight years at that time. While Valliappa was chatting with the bank manager, Chocko asked the security guard if he could see his gun.

The guard indulgently gave it to him. The next moment, there was a ringing shot. Chocko had accidentally fired the gun. The guard had assumed the gun was not loaded. Fortunately no one was hurt, but chaos erupted as people thought a burglary was happening in one of the busiest streets of Bengaluru – Commercial Street.

Valliappa's sons had an eventful childhood. They describe how they were taught the value of frugality early on. Valliappa recalls how in the early day when they owned only one car, and it was otherwise occupied, Seetha Aachi would walk the children home from school uncomplainingly. He proudly points out how well she drove the Fiat and, on occasion, even took the children all the way to Salem.

Valliappa says some of their attempts to instil frugality in their children would come a cropper in the face of indulgent grandparents. 'Thyagu used to love watching car rallies and races and wanted to participate. Seetha and I were worried and refused him permission. Much to our consternation, one day his grandfather gave him ten thousand rupees to go participate in the car rally,' he says.

Recalling those days, Thyagu says, 'My grandfather sponsored me for two seasons and flagged me off without my dad knowing. I was a national rally driver for over fifteen years. My grandfather, who loved cars, vicariously lived the rallying experiences I had.'

Thyagu also talks about Valliappa's relentless spirit – even when the mill was going through tough challenges, Valliappa remained optimistic and encouraged his children to explore other pastures.

'When the mill closed, it could have been a Board for Industrial and Financial Reconstruction (BIFR) case, but my father was particular that all lenders' dues should be given, even if assets had to be sold. His relationship with bankers was such that people were willing to lend,' says Chocko proudly. A quality of his father, he says, was that even his business relationships grew into everlasting bonds.

When Chocko and Thyagu were young, the family travelled widely. A funny incident Chocko recalls is when they had gone trekking in Nepal. His mother lost her footing and took a tumble. Trying to break her fall, Valliappa reached out to hold her and he too fell. 'It was like Jack and Jill tumbling down the hill – and we joke about it like that,' says Chocko. Luckily no limbs were broken.

Chocko's and Thyagu's marriages were arranged by their parents through the usual word of mouth – family circles. Chocko married Coimbatore-based Visalakshi, whose family originally hailed from Rayavaramin Chettinad. They have two children – Valliappa, better known as Valli, and Palaniappan, known as Varun at home. Following the naming traditions of the community, the two were named after their grandfathers, the elder one after the paternal grandfather and the younger one, the maternal grandfather, who was one of the most famous Chettiars of his time, Palaniappa Chettiar, who lived well beyond a hundred. The marriage brought into Valliappa's life a great friend in the form of Visalakshi's father P.L. Subramaniam, who was an investor and banker, and the two hit it off. Now not a day goes by without them chatting on the phone exchanging news.

Thyagu Valliappa married Seetha, the daughter of Mahadevan, a banker who hailed from Devakottai, and they were blessed with two daughters – Krisheetha and Sonakshi. The names of Valliappa's granddaughters were chosen with much care. Krisheetha is derived from Krishna and Seetha, her grandmom, while Sonakshi is an amalgam of Sona and Meenakshi. Thyagu explains, 'The elder granddaughter is supposed to have the grandmother's name. But there were already two Seethas – my mother and my wife and it so happened that I was in Guruvayur when I got news of her birth, so we named her Krisheetha.'

Valliappa's younger daughter-in-law – who shares her mother-in-law's name – has many anecdotes that highlights the affection between husband and wife. She laughingly recounts how every Pongal, which the family celebrates together with great zest, Seetha Aachi would pour a jug of milk on the rice, but Valliappa would chide that she had not poured enough. 'Pour more, pour more,' he would exhort. It's a refrain we hear every year, she chortles.

A beloved member of the Valliappa family was their dog Bozo. The frisky labrador pup came as a gift to Valli, from Thyagu. He brought much joy to the household and lived to the ripe old age of seventeen, well beyond the normal life expectancy of his breed, which is around twelve years. At seventeen, though, he fell ill, and the family vet suggested putting him down. It was a poignant moment for the family. Chocko says, 'I was holding him and literally in a snap of a finger, as soon as the injection was administered on his paw, he fell and passed away.'

Valliappa says, 'I reflected that he lived seventeen years and there were seventeen of us to bid him farewell.'

But the story does not end there. Three years after Bozo died, Chocko was cycling in the Daroji sanctuary near Hampi at sunrise. This was by the banks of river Tungabhadra. Suddenly, an adult labrador came running towards Chocko and clambered on him, wrapping his paws around his neck. 'I started cycling. He followed me. He had a collar. I took him to the resort where my son Varun was sleeping. The dog rushed to him and started waking him up. We gave him a bowl of water and he lapped it up thirstily. Both of us tried to find the dog's owners but nobody in the neighbourhood had seen or heard about him. I contacted the police, who also confirmed there was no report of the lost dog. So we took him back to Bengaluru with us. When we took him to the vet, and asked him how old the dog would be, the vet replied – three years old. It was clear that Bozo had come back to us in a new avatar.'

Since the dog was found in Hampi, whose Lord is called Virupaksha, the Valliappas named the lab Veeran. Veeran truly is a guard dog. His barks would wake the family up many nights.

A Close-knit Unit

At the family dinner table, where traditional Chettinad dishes like mulagu kozhambu or karakozhambu and karamani poriyal or katrikai varuval are always on the menu, one can hear the friendly banter between Valliappa and his grandchildren and sense the affection and strong bonds. The meals at home are simple Tamil fare, whereas in Bengaluru the family dines out often – in earlier days at Koshy's or the Bangalore Club, where Valliappa used to entertain business visitors, and now at fine dining restaurants. Valliappa partakes of strong peppery soups – especially moringa soup – before lunch and dinner. His wife says he prefers steamed snacks to fried ones, while his fitness conscious sons quibble with him over his choice of white rice rather than the healthier red rice. 'In some things, he is very English in his tastes,' exclaim his family.

The pandemic brought the family close. It also earned the youngest granddaughter Sonakshi a nickname – Captain. With an indulgent smile on his face, Valliappa describes how during the lockdown the whole family teamed up into two groups and played many board games together. The teams were divided based on who could not step outdoors during COVID-19 (those under ten and over seventy years of age) and those who had greater freedom. 'So Sonakshi, my wife and I were in one group and Thyagu, his wife and Krisheetha were the other group,' says Valliappa.

Valliappa, the Family Man

For an active, energetic man, the pandemic made Valliappa restless. But his younger daughter-in-law describes how he used the time gainfully, picking up Tamil books and going back to his loved literary volumes. 'He would spend a lot of time in the college library – learning elakiyam [creative] Tamil,' says Seetha. He also used the time to nurture all his connections. 'Every day, he would phone at least four people and chat with them, making sure that he was in touch with all his friends and associates,' she says.

He had long conversations with his grandchildren. 'We heard a lot of family stories from him, and he also recounted many mythological stories of deities,' says Krisheetha. In turn, Valliappa learned to use social media apps from his grandchildren. 'We taught him all about emojis, features on WhatsApp and Instagram,' she says.

Valliappa says he is constantly learning from his grandchildren. He describes how from his two grandsons, Valli and Varun, he picks up new ideas. 'Valli is pursuing his PhD in artificial intelligence in Japan. I call him Professor as he is always studying, and a peer teacher,' he says.

In fact, Valliappa was so fascinated by Valli's peer teaching stint as a student that he introduced it in the Thiagarajar Polytechnic, the Sona College of Technology and the Sona College of Arts and Science. He proudly recounts how Valli got into peer teaching in the first place. When he went to Michigan after his A levels from an IB board school in India, he had 24 credits and needed 124 more credits in his college days. To get these he used to answer a lot of student questions, especially pertaining to maths. At one point, the teacher invited him, 'Would you like to teach?'

'Valli took his teaching seriously. Once we were sitting in a coffee shop with him, when a girl walked in and waved a greeting to him. Is she your classmate, we asked him. No, she is my student, he responded,' says Chocko with a grin.

The vast central library at the Sona College of Technology is also indirectly inspired by Valli. 'When he was doing his undergraduate studies in Michigan, I used to visit him. After dinner, at around 10.30 p.m., Valli would say he needed to go to the library. I was intrigued that so late at night students would be going to the library and was slightly sceptical. One day, I decided to accompany him and was surprised to see how full the library was, and what a stimulating atmosphere there was. At once I decided that I must create something like this at the Sona campus,' says Valliappa.

Indeed, the new library building at the campus is majestic. It's like a centrepiece of the campus – a stately, wide, white building with inviting steps where students can sit around. And it is invitingly open all hours.

As for Varun, who is studying management in Boston, Valliappa picks his brains for marketing ideas for his real estate projects.

Visalakshi talks about what a workaholic her father-in-law was and how he constantly seeks new ideas from unexpected places. 'He is also very bold. He was the very first private citizen in Salem, after the doctors, to get the COVID-19 vaccine at a time when people were nervous about the vaccine,' she says. Similarly, she says, he is bold in his decision-making, never hesitating or overthinking.

'Our father strongly believes in the curative powers of traditional medicine but also embraces modern medicine. His faith in both traditional and modern health practices reflects a deep respect for his roots and a forward-thinking approach to wellness,' says Thyagu.

He is remarkably bold in how he shrugs off the many near-misses he has had, particularly on the road. 'It's as though God is watching over me,' he says. A particularly terrifying incident occurred when he was en route to Salem from Bengaluru in a brand-new Scorpio. Suddenly, the steering wheel of the car just came off. The driver panicked. Valliappa, sitting in the front, was full of horror as the car began hurtling into a tree. However, he kept his composure and immediately applied the handbrake. 'Imagine, we were hurtling at great speed on the highway and there was no way of pulling to the side without the steering wheel. Fortunately, there wasn't much traffic and somehow we managed to stop and hitched a ride back home.' By the grace of God, he says, both were unhurt. But he lost no time in calling the car manufacturer, who agreed to replace the car with an upgraded version.

The very next day, Valliappa fell in the bathroom and fractured his wrist. 'The big accident was averted, but the small accident happened,' he says wryly.

He had another narrow escape when he was in Tirupati, with some relatives. They spent the night at a Bhawan in Tirupati. For some reason Valliappa could not sleep well that night and sat up cross-legged on the bed. Suddenly, the bed went crashing down. 'If I had been lying down, I would have been hurt badly, as it is I only got a shock,' he says, reiterating that he feels a higher presence has been watching over him. He ends the anecdote on a light-hearted note, describing how the hotel wanted to charge them for a broken bed.

Visalakshi describes Valliappa as having extraordinary willpower, unlike anyone she has ever known. As a child, Valliappa had contracted polio, which left him with a limp. But he would never let that hinder his activities and walked a lot. When the ten-storied Sona College of Technology was under construction, and the lifts not yet installed, he would insist on climbing the stairs every day to the terrace. 'He was well over seventy-five, and that's something a younger person would hesitate over – but nothing can stop the chairman,' says M. Adhiyaman, an assistant professor and project engineer in the Department of Civil Engineering at Sona College of Technology, who was closely involved with the building project. 'We never realised how painful walking was for my father-in-law until his doctor told us,' says Visalakshi.

For Valliappa, losing his voice was a big health setback. In 2014, after a minor bout of fever, his throat was badly affected. Initially, he thought it was temporary and just a case of laryngitis. 'I tried everything from Ayurveda to homeopathy to every known home remedy,' says Valliappa. It turned out to be a vocal nerve injury.

For a man who began his day communicating decisions over the phone and who loved public speaking, this was catastrophic. 'His voice was feeble, but still he would try. He did not like to miss any function, and even when he was struggling, he would always take the stage at college and utter a few words of encouragement to students,' says Visalakshi.

Valliappa's belief that there is always a way made him visit several doctors. His friend and mentor Padma Bhushan Professor Rajinder Kumar, a scientist at the Indian Institute of Science, suggested vocal cord surgery. The family set about researching and found that Dr Steven M. Zeitls, director of laryngeal surgery and voice rehabilitation at the Massachusetts General Hospital in Boston, was the best in that speciality. Several leading singers, including Grammy artist Adele, had been to him to work on their vocal pitch.

'We found that the founder of Google, Larry Page, had had the same issue with a vocal nerve injury and was a great supporter of Dr Zeitls. That convinced us,' says Chocko. As an aside, he says, Larry Page told Dr Zeitls, 'Losing the voice has made me a better manager.' 'Why,' asked the doctor? 'I talked less,' was the answer.

The surgery took place in 2015, over a year after his loss of voice. Valliappa says the surgery was done under local anaesthesia and he was aware throughout what was happening. On the surgical table, the doctor asked him to sing to test a pitch. 'I sang a Tamil devotional song. But the surgical team asked me to sing an English song. At that moment I just could not recall anything and recited "Ding Dong Bell". Everybody burst out laughing,' he chuckles.

After the surgery, the first phone call Valliappa made was to Professor Kumar. 'Do I sound the same?' he asked.

An emotional Valliappa says that his family is a lifeline for him. 'My family has always been there to motivate and encourage me to overcome all difficulties in life. The role of every member in my family is unique and important in their own way.'

Perhaps Valliappa has fiercely invested a lot in maintaining harmony in his nuclear family as he has seen a fair bit of discord in his extended family. His cousins have had disputes as have he and his brother.

'The worst moments of my life were when the relationship with my brother broke down, and for a period of time, I was unable to even visit my own mother, who was living in her house, since it was in my brother's possession,' says Valliappa.

After the death of his father, despite a written will directing the division of assets – the educational institutions and Sona Towers jointly to both, the Rajendra Mills in Salem to his brother Sundaram, and the ancestral bungalow to Valliappa – things did not unfold as was willed. His brother retained the house too, citing that it was part of the mill property. Relationships deteriorated to the point where Valliappa's family could not visit the house, and it was deeply traumatic for them. For a period, Valliappa could not even visit his mother. But in 2004, when she passed away, he was by her side. 'She died in my lap,' he says. But Valliappa does not like to dwell on anything sad. This positive outlook tided him over the dark days.

5

Celebrating Eight Rich Decades

In July 2024, there were grand celebrations in Poolankurichi, Salem and Bengaluru. The occasion — Valliappa's sadabhishekam (crossing the eightieth year) and the milestone of sahasra chandra darshanam, the sighting of a thousand full moons, which represents longevity, wisdom and an enriched life journey. This sacred number, connected to the cycles of the moon, is revered in Indian tradition as a marker of a life filled with experiences and divine blessings. Certainly, Valliappa in his eighth decade could reflect with pride and joy on a life filled with rich achievements and wonderful moments.

It was an event planned with great thought and care. Each of the places where the mega celebrations took place symbolised key chapters in Valliappa's life — his childhood, his passion for education and his rise as a business leader.

The festivities began at the historic Lakshmi Vilas Palace, an architectural jewel steeped in Chettiar tradition, where Valliappa nostalgically reconnected with his roots. The guests included local villagers from sixteen nearby communities. The occasion was marked not just by revelry but also by social welfare, including a medical camp led by doctors from Sona Ayush, an initiative driven by Thyagu. It was more than a birthday; it was a celebration of service and breaking bread with the community.

Amid the palace's majestic precincts, the atmosphere was imbued with spiritual depth. The Thiruvasagam performance by the Madurai Women's Forum filled the air with sacred sound, followed by a Ganapati homam, invoking divine blessings for health and longevity. Valliappa's immediate family – Seetha Aachi, Chocko and Thyagu, and their wives and children – were fully involved in the traditional rituals and many of the extended family as well as his beloved college staff arrived from near and far and participated wholeheartedly in the celebrations. The Chettiar characteristic of family unity was in full evidence here.

Nearly a thousand attendees were present at this event, including luminaries from various walks of life, such as M.V. Subbiah, Executive Chairman of the Murugappa Group. Their presence lent joy and blessings to the occasion.

The ceremonies, from the numerous homams ranging from Ganapati homam, Lakshmi homam to Ayush Homam to the gaja puja, were not mere rituals; they symbolised purity, protection and the deep spiritual bond between Valliappa and his family. Of particular significance was the Kalasa Abhishekam, where holy water from the urns were poured on the octogenarian. It is believed that Kalasa Abhishekam boosts the individual's spirituality and brings blessings of prosperity, health and happiness to the family.

This grand celebration of life culminated with the poornakudhi and deeparadhana, ancient rituals that signified the completion of a sacred spiritual cycle.

The celebration's next chapter took place at Sona's Salem campus, where nearly five thousand guests, including students, faculty and the broader community, gathered to honour a man whose name has become synonymous with education. The event opened with a vibrant welcome dance and a pranayama yoga dance performed by children from the Sona Valliappa School, reflecting the enthusiasm and energy that have been integral to Valliappa's vision. This practice, led by Sona Ayush Yogacharyas, an initiative of Thyagu Valliappa, integrates regular yoga routines into students' classroom experience.

Sri Jayendra Puri Mahaswamiji, the peetadhipati of Sri Kailasa Ashram Mahasamsthan, Bengaluru, who has always been a soothing influence in Valliappa's life, delivered a powerful discourse, enriching the spiritual dimension of the event.

A pivotal moment at the event was the release of his biography, *Verum Vizhuthugalum* (Roots and Branches), in Tamil, which chronicles his extraordinary journey through life, education and entrepreneurship. The biography was released by Tamil Nadu's Minister for Urban Development, K.N. Nehru, who presented the first copy to Venu Srinivasan, Chairman Emeritus of TVS Motors and one of the vice chairmen of the Tata Trust, and Dr S.V. Balasubramaniam, chairman of the Bannari Amman Group. Their presence was a testament to Valliappa's far-reaching influence across industries.

The Salem celebration was also attended by vice-chancellors of leading universities, each paying tribute to Valliappa's contributions to education. Among those who joined in honouring his achievements were Dr R. Velraj, vice-chancellor of Anna University; Dr K. Narayanasamy, vice-chancellor of The Tamil Nadu Dr MGR Medical University; and Dr R. Jagannathan, vice-chancellor of Periyar University.

Dr Jagannathan commended Valliappa's transformative approach to education. The remarkable growth and success of Sona institutions stem from their continuous adoption of cutting-edge technologies, he said. This progressive vision has enabled Sona to expand and establish various prestigious institutions, marking a sustained legacy of excellence.

Dr R. Velraj praised Sona College of Technology for emerging among the top ten engineering colleges in Tamil Nadu, attributing this success to Valliappa's visionary leadership. With numerous industrial collaborations, Sona shapes each student's path to excellence, Dr Velraj said, highlighting how these partnerships have become essential to the institution's success.

Padma Bhushan Venu Srinivasan reflected on Valliappa's far-reaching impact, noting that he had profoundly shaped the landscapes of both Salem and Bangaluru. He is known as 'Salem Valliappa' in his hometown and as 'Bangalore Valliappa' in Karnataka – titles that embody his legacy. He admired Valliappa's enduring contributions and offered prayers for his continued service to society for many more years.

Dr S.V. Balasubramaniam shared heartfelt reflections on Valliappa's humility and simplicity, noting that he embodies 'simple living, high thinking'. Valliappa has consistently displayed an uncommon humility by eating the same food as hostel students and using a similar cot during his visits. He added that Valliappa's life offers invaluable lessons for students, parents and young people alike.

K.N. Nehru spoke warmly of Valliappa's contributions, describing how Sona College has become a beacon of pride under his visionary leadership. For any student, gaining admission here is a matter of distinction. His words underscored the institution's impact under Valliappa's guidance.

Former vice-chancellor of Periyar University Dr P. Kolandeivel described how Valliappa's strong commitment towards Indian culture and the well-being of his fellow countrymen has been ably demonstrated time and again. He made particular reference to the COVID-19 period, when Valliappa's generosity was appreciated by the Government of Tamil Nadu, and people of Salem.

The occasion was further honoured by officials and elected leaders from Salem, all recognising Valliappa's profound impact on the region. The event also celebrated excellence across fields, with lifetime achievement awards presented to Dr K. Arthanari of Sri Gokulam Group of Hospitals, R. Chellappan of Swelect Energy Systems, and Sister A.S. Celina Augustine Mary, founder of Lotus Home, for their contributions to health, energy and social service, respectively.

Dr V. Karthikeyan, principal of Thiagarajar Polytechnic College and chairman of the Institution of Engineers (India), Tamil Nadu State Centre shared that the Institution of Engineers (India) has instituted Sri Valliappa Eminent Engineer Award to honour the remarkable contributions of Sri Valliappa in the fields of technical education, industry, innovation and talent development.

The final chapter of this grand celebration unfolded in Bengaluru, where Chamara Vajra Gardens hosted nearly a thousand guests. The elegantly appointed Manikya Hall, with the soothing notes of a live flute performance, created a warm and welcoming atmosphere. Family, friends and dignitaries came together in heartfelt tribute, joined by colleagues from Sona Group institutions and dedicated teams from Vee Technologies, each presence affirming the deep bonds of friendship and respect that have marked Valliappa's journey.

In keeping with tradition, sit-down feasts served on plantain leaves offered guests a taste of Chettinad culinary heritage, while return gifts of traditional sweets and savouries symbolised the family's warmth and commitment to cultural traditions.

Valliappa's sadabhishekam was not just a celebration of age but a reflection on a lasting legacy. His contributions to education, business and philanthropy are woven into the very fabric of the community he has served. This celebration was a testament to the values he has championed: the strength of family, the importance of tradition and an unwavering dedication to excellence – principles that will inspire generations to come.

6

Vyaparam: The 'Can Do' Spirit

A man is but a product of his thoughts, what he thinks, he becomes.

– M.K. Gandhi

THE SEEDS OF enterprise of the Sona Group were sown by Valliappa's grandfather Karumuttu Thiagarajar Chettiar, the philanthropist and activist who founded several textile mills, a bank and many educational institutions. Initially, Karumuttu's forebearers only traded in textiles, but he took the leap into manufacturing, laying the foundation for generations to come.

While Karumuttu's sons inherited most of the mills he founded, it was to his son-in-law Chockalingam Chettiar that he bequeathed the Rajendra Mills in Salem, as well as the Thiagarajar Polytechnic. Chockalingam's family moved to Salem, making it their base, and continued the textile tradition as well as the promotion of education – two things very close to Karumuttu's heart.

In 1964, after graduating from Pachaiyappa's College, Valliappa lived in Salem for two years managing Meena Finance, a financing company that Chockalingam had established, and was trained in the textile business. He revived the stagnant financing company, scaling it, growing it and making it financially healthier. He learned by observing his father closely but developed his own approach too.

Valliappa's first day at work at Meena Finance was unforgettable. He started work on Vijayadashami. He confidently walked into his father's office and sat down opposite him. At this point, his father Chockalingam called the general manager and, pointing to Valliappa, said drolly, 'See, the new managing director has come.' Valliappa says, 'I got the message my father was conveying – I quickly got out of the exalted cabin and sat with the other staff, learning the ropes the hard way.'

While Salem provided the start to his business career, it was Bengaluru where he found his feet and came into his own. A year into his marriage, taking his wife, he headed to Bengaluru with his grandparents' and parents' blessings to set up the Valliappa Textiles that his father had incorporated in 1963 in Ramanagara, with the idea of expanding operations.

When Valliappa's father had first gone to prospect the land for the mill, Ramanagara was a desolate area, says Valliappa. Commuting to the area was tough, and there appeared to be no facilities for workers. He was in two minds, but then he saw a brahminy kite circling over the land, and that convinced him to move forward with the project.

Before the telecom revolution days, communication was difficult. There were no bus facilities and even hiring vans or cars was challenging. Barren land stretched for about ten kilometres on either side of the highway. The mill was constructed within the stipulated time, but it was a challenging task to get operations moving due to a lack of trained technicians. Valliappa threw himself into the challenge and the mill got moving. To attract workers, a school was built and free schooling was offered to their children.

The design of the mill was an architectural or engineering marvel for those days, says Valliappa, as the 120-foot wide and

Vyaparam: The 'Can Do' Spirit

500-foot long hall was pillarless, and the building was made of pre-stressed concrete.

Thyagu mentions that Valliappa was hands on from the very beginning. He grew with the company. He knew every worker in the unit by name. He learned Kannada quickly and could converse fluently with everyone. Chockalingam Chettiar was twenty-six-years old when he started out in business, whereas Valliappa was barely twenty-two when he took on responsibilities in the family business, but he more than managed to live up to his father's expectations.

At its peak, the mill was one of the most productive ones in south India. The mill specialised in fine counts of cotton yarn (from 100 to 140 counts). The quality was good, and most of the goods were exported.

It won one of the top five places in the SITRA (South India Textile Research Association) ranking. The place which was once remote became a famous landmark. Valliappa Textiles became one of the main signposts when travelling to and from Bengaluru. Commuting bureaucrats and politicians became frequent visitors. Among those who dropped in were the deputy commissioner, the local MLA and the Chief Secretary of Karnataka. They were honoured guests at Valliappa Textiles and were treated with warm hospitality. Thus, new friendships burgeoned. The mill became a place that encouraged exchange of ideas. 'Nineteen sixty five to nineteen sixty seven was a game changer for my father,' says Thyagu, recounting the exciting start of the mill.

Valliappa had been well trained by his father. He recalls how particular Chockalingam was about the quality of yarn he produced at Rajendra Mills in Salem. His father would buy only the finest cotton yarn from Egypt for spinning. Once it so happened that the Egyptian cotton was not up to his father's high expectations, although it was passable.

But so quality-conscious was he that he went to the office of the makers of the Sangu Mark lungis and kerchiefs, one of his important customers, to explain the difference personally. Now it so happened that there were two Sangu Mark companies, run by two brothers. One made diamond pattern lungis and the other made square pattern checked lungis to differentiate themselves. 'My father went into the wrong office. The man was very impressed that an MD of the company himself to tell him about such a minute difference. He said, "How come we are not buying from you," and placed an order at once. Thus, my father gained another customer,' says Valliappa.

Even as Valliappa Textiles was spinning along well, the family decided to enter the area of synthetics – a far-sighted move that was ahead of its time – when there were very few synthetic mills. For this, Valliappa set up another company called Sona Synthetics. Valliappa says, 'It became one of the top factories of its time. It consumed a large percentage of Reliance's production of synthetic fibres and Grasim's blended yarns. Reliance supplied fibre to us, and we spun yarn out of it – polyester and polyester viscose.'

But, he says, 'I was against Reliance's policy of setting the price of polyester at the end of the month. I needed to know the price, and only when I had the price could I do the costing. How could I buy something without knowing the price?' This policy of Reliance led him to shift to ICI (Imperial Chemical Industries India).

From inception to execution, the Sona Synthetics plant was completely Valliappa's responsibility. 'I was given total charge of constructing the Sona Synthetics mill. My grandfather Karumuttu Chettiar, in fact, challenged me that I should better my father in the design of the plant,' says Valliappa. So he set about doing just that, creating a

144-feet span building, with structural engineering done by the Indian Institute of Science.

Karumuttu was known for his design sense. Once when he was creating something, he approached a French architect. After spending time discussing the building with him, when Karumuttu asked the architect his fee, he replied, 'A cup of coffee. That's all.' The architect found it so interesting talking to him that he refused to charge. His friends say that Valliappa inherited the same sensibility for design and architecture.

The 1960s and 1970s were a heady period for Valliappa. He read a lot, met a lot of people, kept abreast with the latest trends and boldly embraced the new. For instance, the company started open-ended yarn production. Open-ended yarn was produced by rotors, thus the capacity increased and count was less. 'I installed a lot of twisting machines, doubling machines, and increased capacity with an eye on exports,' says Valliappa.

With the growth in production, the textile mill managed to increase the capacity to one lakh spindles, and business flourished as they could export yarn widely. The area began to be known as 'Valliappa Nagar' in the 1970s.

When anti-dumping cases from Europe threatened the Indian textile industry in the 1970s, Valliappa Textiles was selected as a sample mill that met the stringent quality requirement. Delegates from European nations came and the mill continued to grow thanks to its reputation.

Valliappa, who spent a lot of time on the road, had set a target to buy himself a Mercedes Benz before the age of thirty, and he did. His grandfather Karumuttu visited him on his way to Bengaluru and began quizzing him on his finances, trying to gauge how deep in debt he was. When he learned that Valliappa had no outstandings and was managing the mill profitably, he told him that he was going to send his son Karumuttu T. Kannan to shadow him and learn from him.

'Kannan did arrive. I showed him the mill and took him to various industry associations,' says Valliappa with a grin. The visit cemented the friendship between the two – although Kannan, the son of Karumuttu's second wife, Radha, was technically his maternal uncle (mama), he was ten years younger than Valliappa.

While he worked hands on in the mill and worked hard, Valliappa did not restrict himself to the textiles business but threw himself into activities to promote the industry at large. At the age of forty-three, he became president of the Karnataka Federation Chamber of Commerce, which was founded by Sir M. Visweswaraya in 1916. He was also actively involved in the Karnataka Textile Mill Owners Association where he has been chairman for more than twenty-five years.

Vijay Kumar Yadalam, MD of Ramkumar Mills, says, 'When Mr Valliappa was the chairman of the Karnataka Textile Mill Association (KTMA), I was his vice chairman. One great quality about Mr Valliappa is that he can talk to people without much hierarchy when needed. He can convince people. He can lead without being bossy. Those are good qualities. Especially in industry associations where members are your equal and may even be bigger.'

In Karnataka, for the KTMA, recalls Vijay Kumar, Valliappa was able to prevail upon the government to meet many of the industry's demands. For instance, for a sales tax case, Valliappa's connections with S.R. Bommai, the then chief minister, helped. 'He had good persuasive skills with politicians,' he says.

'Around the time Valliappa became chairman, one major demand among unions was the hike in wages of workers. The kind of hike asked by the unions would have been unsustainable for the mill owners. The government formed a tripartite committee to resolve the issue. It took many meetings to finally arrive at a compromise,' remembers Vijay Kumar.

The Trouble at the Mill

If the late 1960s, saw the blossoming of Valliappa as an able manager and mediator, the 1990s showed his true mettle as a leader who could take tough actions when adversity struck.

The mill business which was spinning wonderfully in the 1970s hit turbulence in the 1990s. With labour costs growing, and many of the subsidies including power withdrawn, it became unsustainable for mills to function. Mills everywhere in the country were threatened but more so in Karnataka as the operations were far from the raw materials.

Meanwhile, at the Valliappa mills, it was a very different issue that spawned labour trouble. Ironically, the trouble came when the textile business was booming, and demand was high. Seeing the demand uptick, the Valliappas had decided to buy more machinery to increase capacity. 'My favourite textile machinery company, Lakshmi Riter (it is now known as LMW), however could not cope and had a waiting time of sixty months,' says Valliappa.

He hit upon a solution. At that time many textile mills in Europe were closing. Valliappa went and bought four factories – one in the Belgium–France border, one in Germany, one near Lake Constance in Austria and one in Mailhos, France – lock, stock and barrel. The idea was to ship machinery from those mills to India, thereby speedily increasing production.

To enable this, they had to borrow heavily, which was not a problem as the textile business was booming so much that banks were falling over themselves to offer Valliappa loans. ICICI executives visited the mills for an on-the-spot appraisal and sanctioned the loan.

The Sona Story

Even as the Valliappas were working on these plans, in Ramanagara, a lot of social and political change was taking place. In 1994, Janata Dal leader H.D. Deve Gowda contested from Ramanagara assembly constituency, moving from Hassan, and became chief minister. During this period, a lot of land deals took place in the constituency. Deve Gowda wanted to attract industries to this area. Among others Toyota, Hindustan and Coca-Cola arrived. And then came the 1996 general elections, for which Deve Gowda contested from Kanakapura constituency, Ramanagara. He became the prime minister of India for a short time.

As the constituency of the chief minister and the prime minister, Ramanagara began attracting a lot of political workers, and the locals began getting involved in unions and party activities. The mill workers at Valliappa's factories too got swayed. They were misled by false promises, says N.S. Raju, who was the head of human resources at the mill.

Motivated by the political climate, the workers' unions went into agitation mode, leading to lockouts, strikes and a suspension of operations for nearly eighteen months. Production decreased and the utilisation of installed capacity reduced significantly. 'Spinning mills require a minimum 90–95 per cent capacity utilisation to break even. Moreover, they could not afford a heavy percentage of use of DG power, which would directly impact profitability. It was a frustrating period as the workers began dictating terms on running of engines. They ruled that the engine could start for running air conditioning but not for production. It became an impossible situation,' recalls Valliappa.

'When trouble comes, it comes in threes,' says Valliappa. There was a major shipment of yarn to Canada, one container for knitting and another for T-shirts. They cost around $200,000 each. The containers looked identical and the

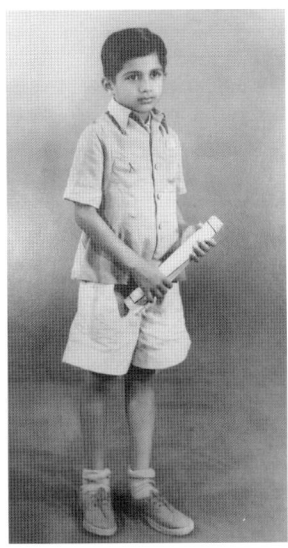

A pampered kid – The youngest sibling, Valliappa was the apple of everyone's eyes

A personable man – Always well dressed, Valliappa cut a dashing figure in his youth

Leading in the leaders – Valliappa, as president of the students' union, had the honour of receiving President Dr Sarvepalli Radhakrishnan and Tamil Nadu chief minister K. Kamaraj

Diverse interests – Valliappa and other students with C.N. Annadurai at the Pachaiyappa's College literary forum meet

Inspiring presence – Valliappa with former president A.P.J. Abdul Kalam, who spent a lot of time at the Sona campus

Friend, philosopher, guide – Valliappa with Padma Bhushan Professor Rajinder Kumar

Visiting luminaries – A young Valliappa along with his father M.S. Chockalingam escorting former president R. Venkataraman

Serious discussion – M.S. Chockalingam, Valliappa and young Chocko with Karnataka chief minister Ramakrishna Hegde

The IT connect – C. Valliappa with former prime minister Rajiv Gandhi

Industry representation – Valliappa with Pranab Mukherjee, finance minister of India

Guest from overseas – Valliappa with the prime minister of UK John Major at an industry chamber meeting

A special equation – Valliappa with prime minister H.D. Deve Gowda

A landmark mill – Vallippa Textiles in Ramanagara was so famous that it served as a major signpost on the Bengaluru–Mysuru highway

Spinning along – Coloured yarn spindles at Sona Synthetics

A prestigious tenant – M.S. Chockalingam with Texas Instruments' Charlie Simon and US ambassador John Gunther Dean at Sona Towers

Much bonhomie – M.S. Chockalingam welcomes the US ambassador as Valliappa looks on

Elegant facade – A view of Sona Towers, Bengaluru, where IT history was made

Symbolic leap – A bullock cart bringing a satellite to Sona Towers

The start of a revolution – The satellite atop Sona Towers

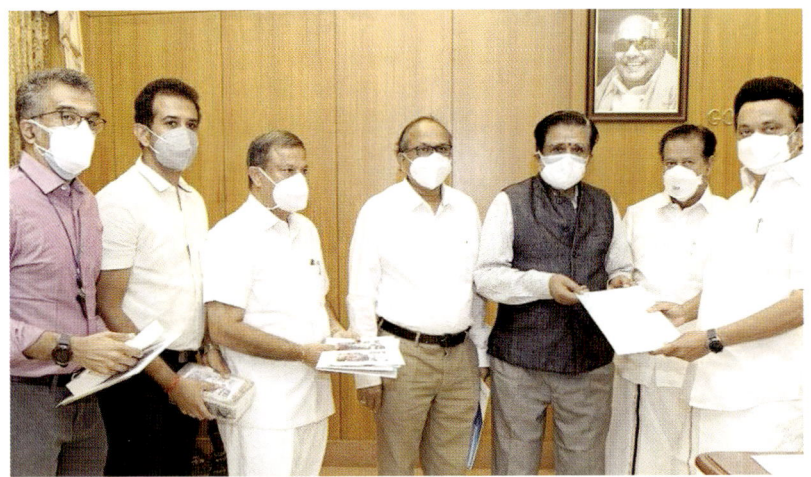

Committed to causes – Philanthropic gestures during the COVID-19 pandemic; with Tamil Nadu chief minister M.K. Stalin

Always positive – Valliappa's endearing quality, as his friends say, is his optimistic outlook

Where it all began – Inauguration of Thiagarajar Polytechnic College

Heritage block – One of the earliest wings at Sona College

Reimagined architectural vision – A wave pattern adorns the main entry of Sona College of Arts and Science

Photo courtesy Sona College of Arts and Science

Standing tall – The state-of-the-art Sona College of Technology building

Inspiring research – The library, open round the clock, is the heart of the campus

New vistas – Valliappa started a mid-rise residential apartment project, Sona Vistaas, at the age of seventy-five

Photo courtesy IMK Architects

College connect – Valliappa addressing students and faculty at the Sona campus

Expanding the campus – Sona Medical College of Naturopathy and Yoga

consignments got mixed up. The factories that were using the yarn did not spot the mistake until it was already in use. It was a nightmarish pickle, he reflects.

Then came a devastating fire. One of the units, which supplied carpet yarn to a factory in Saudi Arabia for prayer mats, had 10 consignments of carpet yarn for Belgium, loaded and waiting. The unions were in a boisterous mood and creating mayhem. Suddenly, the whole unit caught fire. The entire consignment went up in flames. Although insured, the losses were substantial, and only a part of the sum was recovered, and that too after a long time.

As losses mounted between 1995 and 1999, running the factory became unviable. If the fire was grim, what followed was even more devastating – a rasta roko (blocking the road) agitation that turned violent and ended in some tragic deaths. Recalls Thyagu, 'It was as big as Nandigram but there was no social media those days, so the issue was not amplified.'

At the time the unions were constantly in conflict, and a lockout had been declared at the factory. During this time, national elections were in the offing. Between 1996 and 1999, India experienced one of its most unstable political periods, with elections held three times in just two years. Political parties were in perennial campaign mode. Since jobs were an emotive elections issue, Valliappa was approached by some political leaders through emissaries to reopen his mill. He was hesitant because of safety concerns. He was threatened that a rasta roko agitation would be held on the highway and up to the gate of the mill. Since Valliappa remained firm that he would not open the mill without any guarantees of safety and worker compliance, the unions were involved, and the agitation was held. Different political factions turned up and started pelting stones, the agitation suddenly turned violent. Police arrived and began firing. In the melee three people lost their lives and the Hejjala firing of 3 February 1997 made front-page headlines all over India.[1]

It was a tense and fraught time. The Hiremath commission set up to probe the police firing in its findings concluded that the uncompromising attitude of the management and the failure of the Ramanagara authorities to get the agitation banned contributed to the incident. It said the police's contention that it did not give such an order due to election canvassing was an unacceptable excuse.

Valliappa feels that the commission was unduly harsh in its strictures about the management's obduracy considering that a settlement was reached at the labour commissioner's office five times but each time the workers broke it.

The trade union always went back on its promise and would start agitating all over again. They did this because they did not have any stake in the firm. In one of the discussions with the union leaders, Valliappa proposed that he was ready to give terminal benefits to the employees and they could invest in the company and become part owners. However, the union leaders refused this plan, he says.

The mill was finally closed in May 1999 after securing proper permission from the government, though the workers had tried to stall that. 'The mill was closed two months after the death of my father,' says Valliappa.

What hurt Valliappa the most, more than the losses and devastating impact on his business, was the betrayal of his employees. 'My great-grandfather Karumuttu had started as a union leader battling for the rights of tea workers. And later on in his own factories, he was a generous employer,' says Chocko. Valliappa was also pro-worker. 'He would tell workers that they should not work if the air conditioning was off. He would tell them that performance was directly impacted by temperature at work. The provisions for workers were phenomenal,' he says.

At the time they struck work, the workers had received three months' salary as bonus, free schooling for their kids and had the privilege of working on the latest machinery.

'Ironically, the unions held the machinery against us – we had the latest in class, technologically advanced machines. But they said the Davanagere factories had just four machines, and our workload was more as we had more machines. The reality was the opposite, as the Davanagere factories had old machines whereas our machines reduced intensive labour,' he adds.

'Father had built this factory brick by brick. He knew all the workers since they had joined as twenty-year-olds. They grew with him. There was one young lad, whom he had personally mentored and whose training in textiles he had sponsored so that he could grow to be manager. But by then the mill was really scaling and we had to hire experienced leaders to manage operations. The lad took the arrival of the new consultants badly, misunderstanding that his role had been diminished and was a catalyst for the agitating unions,' he recalls, pain in his voice.

The Valliappas felt betrayed when the manager teamed up with the Centre of Indian Trade Union (CITU) union to create trouble in the factory. They say the manager was playing a double game – he thought he would blow out the trouble and earn their goodwill and be promoted. But his game backfired, as the CITU created so much trouble that the mill had to be closed.

'It was painful for our father to see his blue-eyed boy and the employees he had pampered betray him in this fashion,' Chocko adds.

The laws of the land were such that Valliappa's hands were tied. He could not sack any worker. It was difficult to close the company. 'I actually got up and said in one Chamber meeting the Union labour minister attended, "Sir, employing labour is like a Catholic marriage, where divorce is not possible,"' says Chocko, stressing that separation from employees was just not possible those days.

However, they discovered that there was a way. Section 25-O in the Industrial Disputes Act laid down the procedures for closing an undertaking. 'We became the first company to use Section 25-O,' says Chocko.

Vijay Kumar recalls that it was not just Valliappa's mills that faced trouble. There were sixty-six textile mills in Karnataka in the 1980s, but these dwindled to twenty-five by the late 1990s as factory after factory closed.

The closure of the mill was a big setback to Valliappa as there were huge debts to settle. The loans taken to buy the factories in Europe began haunting him. Things were so bad that even the monthly repayments were no longer possible. Valliappa recalls, 'It was an ideal case for BIFR.'

But Valliappa was made of sterner stuff. He shed a lot of assets, machinery and a few apartment projects in Bengaluru that he had started on – Sona Gardens, Sona Residency to name a few – and pledged his coffee estates to make a settlement to workers. The mill itself and the land around was retained. It was later converted into a logistic unit, which incidentally delivered big returns. 'I am making more profit with the logistics unit than I ever did in the textiles business,' says Valliappa.

Chocko remembers, 'We went to our bankers, ICICI Bank, with a view to settle the debts. It so happened that the bank chairman, Mr K.V. Kamath, walked into the room just then. The officials introduced us to Mr Kamath and upon hearing why we were at the bank was impressed with the determination of my father to start something else anew. He was impressed that we did not go to BIFR but wanted to find a way out. He said,

We are looking for entrepreneurs like you.' ICICI then gave some concessions and Valliappa met them more than halfway by pledging assets. 'Today, every banker welcomes my father because of his integrity,' says Chocko.

As the mill business closed, Valliappa advised Chocko to start something in the IT sector. 'What is remarkable about my father is the way he reinvented himself many times. When the textile business he entered as a twenty-one-year-old shut down, he looked forward, investing in a new business,' says Chocko.

In 1995 Valliappa, along with Chocko, then twenty-nine years old, co-founded the incubation company Valliappa Software Tech Park, which acquired the facilities of Texas Instruments when they vacated Sona Towers, and incubated other companies. 'TI had grown so big by then that they were moving to larger offices. They were dumping all the infrastructure we had created for them – the routers, the UPS, etc., and I acquired those and set up an incubation company,' says Valliappa.

While open to new ideas, Valliappa had clear boundaries on the kind of businesses he would support. Chocko recalls how he and a friend, a well-known DJ, got an idea to start a discotheque in Bengaluru. They approached Valliappa for finance. He regarded them both sternly and then said, 'It has taken me more than twenty-five years to establish a reputation as industrialist Valliappa. Now you want me to be called Disco Valliappa?'

In 2000, encouraged by his father, Chocko founded Vee Technologies, a gold standard global services company focusing on revenue cycle management, healthcare and engineering services. In 2024, the company grew to handle transactions of $21 billion annually for global firms with Six Sigma levels of accuracy.

Vee Technologies was set up in Bengaluru, but as it scaled, Valliappa advised his son to create a centre in Salem. Chocko was initially hesitant as he felt Salem might not have the necessary talent needed for the IT outsourcing business, but Valliappa's insistence that it could provide synergies between the group's engineering college convinced him. Today, Salem is among the star performing centres for Vee Technologies. In 2022, Valliappa told Chocko to start an operation around Chettinad. Post COVID-19, a lot of people would love to work from their native places was Valliappa's rationale. Additionally, this would enable them to give back to their native place, an idea Valliappa loved.

The uniqueness of the Salem centre lay in its hiring of women employees, and they were encouraged to work the night shift too. The women were at first concerned about their safety, and they were hesitant to work late hours in the company. But when they were promised a pickup and drop facility, a host of them joined. The location of the centre proved to be an inspired choice as many of the graduating tech students from Salem loved the idea of working in their own city. Vee Technologies turned out to be a great source of employment for many students from the region. Today Sona College of Arts and Science is the go-to destination for Vee's Salem centre, especially for hiring fresh biotechnology and science graduates.

Meanwhile, Valliappa was pursuing other avenues. He ventured into a chemicals business, with the idea of producing copper sulphate. The idea came after meeting the Padma Bhushan scientist Professor Rajinder Kumar, who was then chairman of the Department of Chemical Engineering at IISc at that time. copper sulphate is made by mixing sulphuric acid and copper scrap. 'For this we took copper ore from a copper company in Chitradurga, and we roasted it in a fluidised bed. It's a difficult process. We then mix it with sulphuric acid and extract copper,' explains Valliappa.

Vyaparam: The 'Can Do' Spirit

Under the guidance of Professor Kumar, the production commenced and was successful, but it could not grow as a business due to price fluctuations and changes in government policies. Valliappa says, 'Though the business was a loss, I gained a valuable lifelong mentor in Professor Kumar. He was a big strength to us, even for our college.' From the selection of the principal to pressing issues related to students, Valliappa would take advice from Professor Kumar. Indeed, for even personal issues, Professor Kumar was his go-to adviser.

Taking the ups and downs in business and always seeing the bright side was a characteristic of Valliappa.

Some business expansions happened consciously, others through serendipity. For instance, Lal Bagh Coffee Estate happened by sheer accident. Valliappa's father had bought an estate in Yemmigoondi in 1972. 'There is a history to Chettiars picking up coffee estates,' says Valliappa.

In India, in the late 1950s and 1960s, the coffee companies in Coorg, which were predominantly owned by the British who used to export the beans, began attracting heavy taxation from the government. The English found the business unsustainable and began exiting, many of them selling to Chettiars, who had gone to Singapore and Malaysia wanted to come back to India. 'Many of these sale deals happened in Singapore and Malaysia – it was understood that if a Chettiar gives a word, they keep it,' says Valliappa.

Somehow, whenever a prime estate came up for sale in Coorg, the brokers would reach out to the Chettiars first. It was thus that in 1979 a close associate and great well-wisher of Valliappa's father – Arthur Coloso – asked another prominent Chettiar based in Salem, M.A. Palaniappan, to check out an estate of a thousand acres called Lalbagh in Chikkamagaluru on the Baba Budangiri mountain range.

Incidentally, when Karumuttu Thiagarajar had acquired Rajendra Mills in Salem, it was Palaniappan's family that acquired the Jawahar Mills. Palaniappan asked Valliappa's father to help him with the transaction.

This estate belonged to an Englishman named Edward White, whose father had made himself at home in the Scotland of the East, buying up estates in the area. White's father bought a rubber estate in 1927 for a sum of ₹25,000 to be paid in five instalments and held it till 1948. While most British owners of the coffee estates in Coorg and Chikkamagaluru returned to their soil post-Independence, White's father stayed on, consolidating his estate. He worked parallelly in other estates as a manager and those days estate managers were often given shares in the company. When the companies left India, these managers eventually became the owners.

Arthur Coloso got White and Valliappa's father to meet at a hotel in Bengaluru to negotiate the deal and Valliappa went along. 'The talks went on for long – White and Coloso took drinks while we drank Fanta,' says Valliappa. Meanwhile, Palaniappan had backed out – he was having some problems with his mill and did not want to plunge into the coffee business at such a time. But Valliappa's interest had been aroused and he told his father he would like to buy the estate. 'My father thought the thousand-acre estate would lead to low income for seven years and it was too big for him to chew. He told the agents, my son says he can do it in a shorter time,' recalls Valliappa. For Valliappa buying the estate was an act of courage. The talks went on for over six hours and at midnight the deal was closed.

After that the whole family drove down to see the estate, one sunny day in 1979. Interestingly, the same estate was being looked over by Visalakshi's parents as they owned a property nearby. When they approached White with the intention of

Vyaparam: The 'Can Do' Spirit

buying it, he told them it was already sold. 'They were shocked to learn that without seeing it my father had bought it,' chuckles Chocko, adding that his father could be very quick and decisive.

Many of the real estate deals were arranged by Coloso and his friend Stevie Mathias who were constant visitors to the Valliappa home and became good friends of the family.

Years later, Chocko acquired a coffee estate in Polipeta, near the Tata Coffee property, from the Reddy family that runs a large healthcare chain in the country. That deal, he says, took just three and a half minutes to close. 'I think the family trait is quick deals,' Chocko chuckles.

Valliappa points out that they could close land deals quickly as they empowered their land agents to act. He recounts how they were buying an estate in Chikkamagaluru for their younger sister Kamala from a European. 'We were busy with a wedding in the family. Arthur Coloso came to us and said the deal had to be closed immediately as the owner was going abroad. I handed him my Jeep and a blank cheque and told him to go ahead.'

Later, says Valliappa, Coloso told him that when he was trying to close the deal, the European was highly sceptical whether he was empowered to do it. At which point Coloso showed him the blank cheque and also the Jeep key and said, 'Here is their car key, I have been driving it, and I have been given total authority.'

A side to that story is that Coloso, a jovial large-built Mangalorean a long moustache, drove that jeep all over beautifully but rammed it into Valliappa's house gate when he was returning it. Coloso was a great favourite of the family, and he would often drop in to taste Seetha Aachi's idlis, which he was very fond of.

Valliappa's estate shows better productivity than that of seasoned coffee growers, says Chocko. 'That's because my father approaches everything precisely. Every morning at seven sharp, he is on a fifteen-minutes call to the estate manager and he knows every bush on the estate,' he says. The mother plants have been chosen with great care. Some of these plants yield 50,000 fruits annually. Normally, a plant only yields about 20,000 fruits. 'Now the Coffee Board is developing tissue culture from those plants,' he adds. The plantation also keeps beehives – and Valliappa thinks they help in increasing the yield.

Even in the coffee estate, Valliappa is trying bold experiments. For instance, he is trying to use mushroom-based fertilisers from one of Sona Group's research projects.

Abreast of all latest trends, Valliappa had also decided to get into biotech with the launch of the Mycelium Sona Biotech (MSB). The first laboratory was set up in Salem in association with the Australian company Mycelium. 'The idea behind Mycelium Sona Biotech is to produce mushroom extracts and study its uses in medicine and agriculture,' says Valliappa, who is the biggest user of Sona Mycelium products, experimenting with it on his estate.

In 2003, the forward-looking Valliappa also ventured into the field of electrical machine by launching Sona SPEED (Sona Special Power Electronics & Electric Drives), recognising an opportunity in electrical machines. It began in the R&D labs of Sona College of Technology and was established by Valliappa to bid for the global tenders for the supply of Space and Military grade motors. Sona SPEED has already played a role in the Chandrayaan-3 mission, for which it built a stepper motor that was used in the Launch Vehicle Mark III.

But for Valliappa, his most personally satisfying diversification has been into real estate. His eye for spotting prime land deals, married with his passion for architecture, makes him adept at creating winning real estate projects. Soon after the success of

Sona Towers, he put up a few small projects, but then the textile business consumed so much of his energy and then the debts had to be paid off. Of course, all the constructions – whether personal homes or the buildings for his various businesses – were under his supervision.

However, at age seventy-five, when all was even keel with his other businesses, he turned his eye again on real estate, lovingly creating the Sona Vista as residential project off Bannerghatta Main Road in Bengaluru. Spread over ten acres, the low-rise colony with green pockets, beautiful landscaping, a club house with swimming pool and gym is like an oasis near the Electronic City. Valliappa roped in Rahul Kadri for the project and says he had great fun being involved in a project he knew would resonate with the IT workers. The housing units were kept deliberately compact, targeting young couples, the highlight being the swank club house and the stunning central gardens, with a terraced green common area.

Active in Industry Associations

Alongside his business ventures, Valliappa made time for industry association meetings. He had a thirty-year innings as president of Karnataka's Textile Mills Association (KTMA). In the beginning, the association had limited funds, and it functioned only on the mercy of the association members. During his tenure, Valliappa streamlined the treasury through some active fundraising, strengthening the asset base of the association to ₹15 crore.

At the age of forty-three, he became president of the Federation of Karnataka Chamber of Commerce and Industry (FKCCI). The story of how he became president is an interesting one. The chamber was dominated by business groups that were into trading, while the manufacturers had scarcely any representation in the leadership. K. Shiva Shanmugham, who ran Shivashakti Engineering Works producing steel barrels for the petrol industry, described how the industry captains requested Valliappa to stand for election.

'He won with a big margin and brought great change in the association,' says Shanmugham. Many IAS officers heading Karnataka state corporations turned up for voting and helped Valliappa win. 'Till he took charge, it was a trade-dominated chamber. Only when Valliappa took over in 1988 did the industrialists begin joining. That is how the industry captains came to be involved. He wrought great change and made the industry – small, medium, big – wake up, and because of the strength of representation we could make demands from the government,' he says. Incidentally, Valliappa became the youngest president of FKCCI, a chamber which is now over a century old.

This was an exciting time for Valliappa, who loved meeting people. 'It's the best way to learn – you meet people, you hear new things and absorb new ideas,' he says. A particularly exciting trip was a month-long immersion in the US as part of an India–US visitor's exchange programme. 'One politician and one industrialist from India visited the US every year. In one of the trips, Tamil Nadu chief minister MGR too had been a member,' he says. Valliappa went in 1990, and since he evinced interest in seeing textile mills, he got to visit South Carolina and North Carolina. 'We were also taken to the White House and given VIP treatment everywhere,' he says. A memory that still enchants him is the visit to the currency printing press in Washington.

Buoyed by all he had seen and absorbed, he infused dynamism in the FKCCI, taking teams to Australia, New Zealand, Singapore and Malaysia to gather ideas on how industries should be functioning. Further, to empower women he organised seminars exclusively for women at Coorg with the help of some principal industrialists from Karnataka.

'The motivation he gives to young entrepreneurs is tremendous. He has a beautiful vision. When we attend board meetings with him, we learn a lot – he often tells us, don't go for short term, but look at the long term,' says Shanmugham.

He shares an insight into how Valliappa thinks about business. Once a huge consignment of steel had to be ordered for which Valliappa arranged large trailers for transportation. Someone raised an objection pointing out that the lengthy trailer would not be able to pass through the compound, while a lorry could. 'Valliappa thought for a minute. He calculated that the lorry could carry only fifteen tonnes or so of material whereas the lengthy trailer could carry forty tonnes, and in all savings of four lakh rupees would be achieved by opting for a trailer. He said, break the compound wall, allow the trailer to pass and rebuild it, it will be cheaper.' It was such an out-of-the-box solution, says Shanmugam admiringly.

When it comes to numbers and accounting, Valliappa has the most amazing memory. Once his grandfather Karumuttu had said about Chockalingam, 'Even when he is enjoying near Marina Beach and someone suddenly asks him about the figures in his company, he can rattle them off.' Similarly, Valliappa can remember phone numbers without aid. In fact, often he remembers the number and matches them to the name rather than the other way round.

Given his skills in representation to the government, industry bodies sought Valliappa. Four years after he became FKCCI president, he was asked to take over the Bangalore Chamber of Industries and Commerce (BCIC). The office bearers said, 'Valliappa, you have the experience, you take over.' 'I became the chairman unanimously,' Valliappa says.

The Sona Story

Years later, his son Thyagu became the youngest president of BCIC in 2016–2017.

T.R. Parasuraman, Toyota's executive adviser and a former president of BCIC, says, 'Despite their disagreements, people are drawn to Valliappa and are willing to pay attention to his thoughts,' he says.

When Thyagu's tenure at BCIC ended, Valliappa asked Parasuraman to accept the position of president. 'I was reluctant, but Valliappa persuaded me by pointing out the many ways in which I could make a difference, especially by facilitating business exchanges between India and Japan.'

'I can't help but think of a Japanese adage to fit Valliappa – outstanding people produce outstanding products,' he says.

In 1995, Valliappa was elected president of the Bangalore Management Association, one of the oldest associations in India. Thyagu is also a keen follower of management trends. As president of the Madras Management Association (Salem chapter), Thyagu launched a pathbreaking initiative: a series of programmes aimed at management students, offering valuable knowledge, skills and insights to prepare them for successful management careers. Enriched through networking and collaboration, this learning experience, Thyagu believes, will help create better leaders in the field.

Apart from industry associations, Valliappa was also actively involved in his own community activities as chairman of Nagarathar Association, Bengaluru. For a short while, he was also president of the All-India Copper Sulphate Manufacturers Association. Additionally, he was president of Employer Federation of South India (EFSI) which covered the four states of Tamil Nadu, Kerala, Karnataka and Andhra Pradesh. 'I was there for two terms,' he says. 'Chakravarthi Rajagopal of Amco batteries urged me to take over,' he recalls. 'I was also president of the Air Passengers Association of India,' he chuckles. Thyagu also became president of EFSI for a brief while.

Srinivasa Ayyangar Sampathraman, a director at D.P.K. Engineers Private Limited, who has known Valliappa for over thirty-five years, says bargaining is customary in business, but Valliappa conducts it fairly. He says, when it comes to business, Valliappa keeps it extremely professional. He recounts an incident when Valliappa took a quote for a diesel genset. After some days when Sampathraman asked him what happened, he said he had found somebody else supplying it cheaper and purchased it from them. 'But I could have reduced the rate for you – you did not give me a chance,' protested Sampathraman. Valliappa told him he should not do so on the basis of friendship, and if he could have given at a better rate, he should have said so right at the beginning itself.

Sampathraman also once told Valliappa that he could supply furniture to his Sona colleges. 'If you can do it, so can I,' retorted Valliappa, at once asking the mechanical engineering department to try their hand at it. Now the entire production of furniture for Sona colleges is in-house.

Although an immigrant to Karnataka, Valliappa has worked more for the welfare of the state, than most, says Shanmugham. Valliappa says Bengaluru has fulfilled his vision as an entrepreneur. He describes how the nameplates of all his businesses are in Kannada.

In honour of Bharat Ratna Sir M. Visveswaraya's birth anniversary, the Institution of Engineers India, Tamil Nadu State Centre, instituted the annual 'Valliappa Eminent Engineer Award'. This tribute not only celebrates Sir Visveswaraya's visionary legacy but also acknowledges his founding of FKCCI, an organisation that Valliappa passionately led in 1988 and continues to contribute to. Today, Valliappa is revered as a guiding father figure, whose wisdom and experience are sought after to resolve complex issues, keeping the spirit of Sir Visveswaraya's ideals alive. The hallmark of Valliappa's long innings as a business magnate is his impeccable reputation as an upright administrator. All rules are followed meticulously and uniformly for everyone. At the same time, Valliappa is not scared of taking risks. 'Every business is a risk, real estate more so. But if it clicks, it clicks well,' he says.

Sampathraman quotes a Thirukkural couplet to describe Valliappa's nature.

This man, this work shall thus work out,' let thoughtful king command;
Then leave the matter wholly in his servant's hand.

Couplet No. 517

7

Seeding Knowledge: Institution Building

As one drives into Salem, one gets the feeling of being in a natural amphitheatre. This beautiful town in Tamil Nadu is nestled amid picturesque hills. The name Salem is derived from 'Sela' or 'Shalya' which means 'surrounded by hills'. Today the town is variously referred to as Steel City, Agro City, Limestone City, Electric City and Mango City – forming the acronym SALEM!

For the Valliappas, this is their first home, the place where their business journey began. They are fiercely proud of the town and its heritage, and they are doing their bit to add to its iconicity.

'Did you know that Salem district was the first district to be formed in south India?' says Valliappa. In 1790, Salem was established as a district encompassing Namakkal, Dharmapuri and Krishnagiri. The 'Collectors of Salem' wooden plaque displayed at the Salem Collector's office lists Mr Kindersley as the first district collector, serving from 30 November 1790 to 3 April 1792. Over the past 234 years, 174 officers have served as collectors in Salem.

Located on the foothills of the Yercaud hills, Salem is known as the sago capital of India and is the gateway to many cities in Tamil Nadu, including Erode and Tirupur. The town is also famous for its handlooms and silver anklets.

In recent years, the town has become a recognised education hub. The clock tower of the ten-storeyed Sona College of

Technology stands as a noteworthy landmark. On the sprawling 47-acre Sona campus, over 12,000 students, ranging in age from 4 to 60, study as the Valliappa group continues its mission to provide quality education in this tier-2 town.

From a polytechnic set up in 1958 to a campus with multiple institutes providing education in a variety of domains, the story of the Sona campus's growth and the Valliappa group's expanding footprint over the city is inspiring.

Step into the verdant campus, and you are met with the sound of chirping birds, occasionally pierced with the raucous caws of crows, and the bustling chatter of students rushing from one class to another. It is hard to imagine that this vibrant campus once faced its share of power struggle and challenges before finding order.

The oldest building on the Sona campus is the Thiagarajar Polytechnic College. Among the 3,500 polytechnic institutes in the country, Thiagarajar Polytechnic consistently ranks at the top spot in AICTE-CII surveys for its industry-linked programmes.

Thiagarajar Polytechnic has a fascinating history. It was set up by Karumuttu Thiagarajar Chettiar when India had few technical education institutions (the British prioritised the growth of arts colleges over colleges dedicated to technical knowledge). The government had asked industrialists to step up. Recognising the importance of education in fostering holistic economic development, Thiagarajar Chettiar plunged into the task of building a technical institute.

The last governor general of India, lawyer, activist, statesman, Salem's own C. Rajagopalachari played a pivotal role in the early days of the institute. Classes began in his house before the foundation of the institute was laid on the Sona campus in 1958. It took two years to complete the building that Thiagarajar Chettiar envisioned, and till then classes were held at Rajaji's home.

Seeding Knowledge: Institution Building

'We took his house and put a thatched shelter, and we started civil, mechanical and electrical departments with one hundred and twenty students. Next year we expanded to one hundred and sixty by adding textiles,' recalls Valliappa.

The inauguration of the polytechnic was graced by key leaders such as the then Union minister for education, K.L. Shrimali, the then minister for industries of Madras state, R. Venkataraman, and the then UGC chairman, Humayun Kabir.

The building Karumuttu created was a charming colonial-style structure with greenery in every corner — his trademark style that remains evident on campus to this day. 'My grandfather had an eye for architecture and each of the buildings he created had a distinctive stamp,' says Valliappa.

Valliappa has an equal flair for architecture. He has expanded the campus keeping the character of the traditional, heritage buildings intact even as they have been modernised. The newer buildings introduce a strikingly different style, creating a unique blend of colonial charm and contemporary design.

The Early Days

When Thiagarajar Polytechnic was established in the late 1950s, Karumuttu realised the need of the day was for civil, mechanical, electrical and electronics, and textile engineers. The institute proceeded to offer courses in these areas. At the time, the Nehru government was focused on setting up manufacturing public sector undertakings (PSUs), creating a significant demand for skilled workers in a number of fields.

Significantly, the Thiagarajar Polytechnic was the first institute in south India to admit female students for technical courses. Until 1976, the college's Technical Diploma programmes were open only to male students. During that time, the Central and state governments launched schemes to offer opportunities for women to pursue technical education. As part of the initiative to increase opportunities for women in technical education, Valliappa's father, Chockalingam decided to admit female students.

In keeping with the times, Chockalingam also expanded the engineering streams into areas like computers and production in the 1980s. Thiagarajar Polytechnic was one of the earliest institutions to introduce computer programmes, taking advantage Rajiv Gandhi's computer policy of 1984. 'We got a grant to introduce an IT curriculum in the polytechnic,' says Valliappa.

It was an exciting time for the institution. In 1991 under Valliappa's guidance the college launched several community development programmes. A year earlier, the Canada India Institutional Cooperation Project (CIICP), a major human resource development project, had selected Thiagarajar Polytechnic for its first centre in India. CIICP transformed the polytechnic college into a hub for community education.

Chocko recalls, 'As part of a Commonwealth Initiative in 1989, the Canadians agreed to share the best practices in community education with India. The Canadians wanted to work with the best polytechnic in India and luckily TPT got selected. As part of the training, a team from TPT went to Canada to learn the latest in community education.' Chocko himself visited New Brunswick Community College, which he says was like travelling to the North Pole.

One key recommendation made by the Canadian experts was that 70 per cent of the academic council should be from industry. Once the training was completed, the TPT faculty were entrusted with implementing the practices first in Salem and across Tamil Nadu, and later expanding the initiative to Maharashtra and Rajasthan.

Seeding Knowledge: Institution Building

The overall objective of the project was to enable people to hone their skills in multiple areas through part-time, area-relevant courses. For instance, gold appraisal was among the trades that the authorities and the appraisers benefited from.

The five-year alliance with the Canadians left a lasting impact on Thiagarajar Polytechnic, making it extremely community-focused. The experience also inspired Valliappa to embrace forward-thinking ideas on delivering education to those whom it could not reach.

For instance, in 1993, Valliappa established the Continuing Education Centre at Thiagarajar Polytechnic. One lakh students benefited through the 6,413 non-formal and short-term skill development programmes offered by the CIICP.

Valliappa was determined to train the underprivileged rural youth and women. The Community Development through Polytechnics scheme, a Ministry of Education project, was established to achieve this goal. This initiative enabled around 25,000 rural youth to set up on their own emerged.

The courses offered included mushroom cultivation and beauty training. The mushroom cultivation course came about because the trainers discovered that whenever women earned money, they would hand over the money to their husbands, who squandered it all on alcohol. This led to the idea of training women in a vocation that would provide them with sustenance and income. The women could grow the mushrooms and use them to prepare their daily meals.

One of the beneficiaries of this programme was Prabha Reddy from Karur, who travelled 100 kilometres for the beauty training courses. She was vocal about the need for beautician training skills in villages pointing out that there was huge aspiration among rural women. She went on to become an entrepreneur with a ₹100 crore beauty training business.

Changing Perceptions

A challenge several polytechnics face is that diplomas for vocational courses they offer are not as respected as those from institutions that offer graduate programmes. But the Thiagarajar Polytechnic managed to conquer that perception as the students graduating from the institute got great placements, while others treated it as a bridge course to higher studies. A significant proportion of the students pursue a degree course after completing their diploma programme or midway through it. Interestingly, engineering colleges offer lateral entry to diploma students, allowing them to join in the second year. 'Sixty per cent of students passing the institute go for jobs, while the rest opt for higher education,' says Dr V. Karthikeyan, the principal. 'We have taught more than fifty thousand students.'

Several of Thiagarajar Polytechnic's alumni have become renowned entrepreneurs. For instance, R. Chellappan, the founder and MD of Swelect Energy Systems, achieved considerable success. After studying at the polytechnic, he went on to do an engineering degree and founded Numeric Power Systems, an energy business, which he sold to the French company Legrand for a substantial sum. He attributes his success to his early training at the polytechnic, where his course may have cost less than ₹800 a year.

Many students went on to become managing directors of textile mills and civil contract companies. TPT has also provided skilled talent to auto manufacturers like the TVS group and Ashok Leyland. Incidentally, four of Ashok Leyland's top five team members are TPT alumni. The TPT principal, Dr Karthikeyan, is a product of the institute himself. He notes, 'About forty per cent of our staff members are our alumni.'

In 2019 the institute, which had been showing great agility in adding new courses based on industry needs and regional demands, was chosen by All India Council for Technical

Education (AICTE) as a mentor institute – a significant honour. It now provides guidance to scores of other polytechnics in the country to help them improve.

As a mentor institute it has guided over a hundred polytechnics and fifty engineering colleges on how to increase their students' learning capabilities. 'We shared our innovative educational practices with them,' Dr Karthikeyan says.

For the silver jubilee of the polytechnic, in 1983, the then Union defence minister R. Venkataraman, who later became vice president (1984–87) and then president of India (1987–1992), graced the inauguration ceremony of TPT. For the golden jubilee in 2008, President A.P.J. Kalam was the guest of honour. During his visit, he also spent considerable time at the Sona College research centres.

Engineers of Tomorrow

In 1995, there was a growing demand in Salem for an engineering college. 'Most students from the city who were dreaming of doing engineering were going to Bangalore or Chennai or Coimbatore or Trichy. There was a gap,' says Professor S.R.R. Senthilkumar, the principal of Sona College of Technology.

Chockalingam Chettiar decided to fill the gap by setting up the Sona College of Technology within the Sona campus in 1997. The college began with three departments and 180 students. From the germ of the idea, Valliappa was involved in the engineering college project, working closely with his father.

The Nagarathar community has long been committed to the education cause. Raja Sir Annamalai Chettiar founded the Annamalai University. Vallal Alagappa Chettiar founded the Alagappa College. Sevagan Annamalai Chettiar founded the Sevagan Annamalai Arts College. Karumattu Chettiar played a key role by setting up the greatest number of education institutions in Madurai including the Thiagarajar College of Engineering, Thiagarajar School of Management, Thiagarajar College and Thiagarajar Model Higher Secondary School. There are around 150 schools founded by Nagarathars. They have established schools at all levels – middle schools, high schools and higher secondary schools – in more than 65 villages. In a way Valliappa and his father were not only carrying the legacy of Karumuttu forward but they were also emulating the stalwarts in their community.

However, it was easier said than done. In India, the landscape for private educational institutes is challenging. Education is a highly regulated sector. In 1983, the MGR government in Tamil Nadu allowed private-sector colleges through the self-financing route for the first time.

For the entrepreneurs looking to set up self-financed private engineering colleges it was a catch-22 situation. Building a college, especially an engineering institute with state-of-the-art lab facilities and equipment, is expensive. However, the student fees were insufficient to recover the costs. This is when colleges began charging substantial capitation fees. It snowballed into a huge issue and the government began regulating the sector more.

In 1997, when the Sona College of Technology was created, Valliappa wanted to take the self-financing route. Chockalingam was reluctant as he was running an aided polytechnic. But Valliappa pointed out that contexts had changed and that it was no longer feasible to start an aided institute. Despite their differences, both father and son agreed that the focus should not be on making money from education but on contributing to national development through the dissemination of knowledge. Valliappa says that for too long youth had to go to metro cities for quality higher education. With the Sona College of Technology, the goal was to provide this education right at their doorstep. The vision was to make the college an institution of great repute in the fields of science, engineering, technology and management studies so as to attract students from smaller cities as well. Thus, Sona offered a full range of programmes of global standard – from undergraduate and postgraduate to doctoral programmes in engineering, technology and business.

However, setting up the college faced opposition within the family. Valliappa's elder brother, Sundaram, was not at all keen on the expansion, while Valliappa himself was enthusiastic. Finally, Chockalingam told Valliappa to obtain the necessary government approvals – if he succeeded, they would proceed. Fortuitously for Valliappa, S.R. Bommai, whom he knew from his chamber activities in Bengaluru, was the Union human resource development minister. After following the proper processes and ensuring the merits of the case, the approvals came through quickly. To help set up the engineering college, Valliappa brought in Dhiraj Lal Gandhi, who had retired as the principal of Thiagarajar Polytechnic, to serve as the college's secretary. However, over time Lal's personal ambitions diverted his attention from his role at the Sona College of Technology. 'That's because he was setting up his own engineering college in Salem,' says Chocko, describing the obvious conflict of interest.

He then describes how his great-grandfather Karumuttu once faced a similar situation. C.S. Ramachari, who worked with him in the textile business at Meenakshi Mills and was a trusted aide, wanted to start a textile company of his own, even as he worked with Karumuttu. But Karumuttu firmly told Ramachari that he could not work in his mill while starting a competing company. 'In hindsight, perhaps we should have followed his example and not allowed Dhiraj Lal the leeway of doing both,' says Chocko. But Valliappa reasons that given the circumstances – when his brother Sundaram was creating impediments too – they had to take a softer approach.

The Sona Story

A major confusion created by Dhiraj Lal involved student placements. Early on, Sona College of Technology had tied up with a top recruiter to visit the campus and exclusively choose students from the campus. Three hundred students – nearly 50 per cent of the college's batch – would be absorbed by this recruiter, a leading consulting MNC. However, when the arrangement faltered, there was chaos and the college had to scramble to form new partnerships for placements. 'In hindsight it was a good thing that happened,' says B. Saravanan, the director of placements at the college. Thanks to Valliappa and Chocko using their connections, the college could attract over 300 companies to conduct campus recruitment drives. 'We expanded the opportunity for students,' says Saravanan.

Chocko agrees. 'Thanks to this crisis, we also created a new company called HireMee, which maps how job-ready students are.'

Thyagu describes how further advancements were made in the placements by developing a robust tech system, by inviting CEOs to the college to build industry–academia connections and by introducing sectoral placements.

Meanwhile, the college continued making progress. From the beginning Valliappa, a great believer in thinking long-term, was insistent that Sona College of Technology should offer courses of the future and focus a lot on R&D. That paid off. As Senthilkumar proudly points out, 'Sona College of Technology is today in the sky and in the deep sea.'

The college's Sona SPEED R&D division and the Sona PERT (Power Engineering Research and Testing) centre have taken it sky-high and ocean-deep. At the Sona SPEED lab, housed in the main building of the college, a twelve-member team made up of faculty and research scholars developed crucial components that powered the Chandrayan-3 Moon Mission. Just a few hundred metres away from the Sona PERT centre,

Sona SPEED has developed solutions that have powered deep sea mining missions.

'For the world's thinnest watch made by Titan Industries, we have given nano coating,' says Senthilkumar. Between 2019 and 2024, the college has earned 38 patents out of the 162 patents application filings. These range from an unusual sweat transfer tester which helps fabric makers understand how materials handle perspiration to magnetically treated water to help in sustainable agriculture by enhancing absorption of minerals in soil, thereby doing away with the need for fertilisers.

Sona's students are making a deep impact not only in scientific research but in management and entrepreneurship too. Shiva Shanmugham, a past president of FKCCI, shares that the association's Manthan contest for young entrepreneurs, where students across south India are asked to send in their ideas, saw students from Sona College and Thiagarajar Polytechnic placing second, fourth and fifth in 2021. The prize money is ₹2.5 million and the contest is judged by IAS officers. 'What surprised me was those students from Sona College and Thiagarajar Polytechnic were placed second, fourth and fifth in 2021, the first year it was opened to colleges outside Karnataka. One does not expect students from a small town like Salem to beat students from big metros like Chennai, Hyderabad and Bengaluru. The fact that students got three prizes for turning in excellent business ideas is amazing, and the credit goes to Valliappa.' The registration fees for the contest were funded by Valliappa to encourage the students.

Shanmugham says, 'Valliappa is concerned about skilling youth. He says, by 2028, youngsters will be nearly 50 per cent of our population and it is up to us to shape their future and educate them.'

At the Sona School of Management, participation in the 'Speakers Forum' has led the MBA student teams to excel in several business quiz competitions of repute. These include many wins at the Tata Crucible Business Quiz as well as the National Business Quiz at a leading regional engineering college, adds Thyagu.

Focus on R&D

A constant concern in academic circles in India has been the lack of research mindset and the Sona College of Technology has been addressing this concern from the beginning. Shares Senthilkumar, 'There are thirty-six R&D centres in Sona College, showing how highly the institute is focused on research.'

The research journey at Sona was blessed by none other than the then president of India Dr A.P.J. Abdul Kalam. A high point in the college's journey was having the forward-thinking president inaugurate its R&D centres.

Dr Kalam was so engaged during his visit that he spent four hours exploring the college's R&D centres. Inaugurating the virtual e-learning A-view (Amrita Virtual Interactive E-learning World) facility, Dr Kalam went online with Dr P. Venkat Rangan, the vice-chancellor of Amrita University, Coimbatore, demonstrating how specific concepts could be delivered virtually.

At the time, only premium institutes like the IITs had A-view facilities, which facilitated lectures from specialists to be delivered from any place at any time on any subject. This system addressed a significant issue in higher education in India – the shortage of highly qualified teachers – by allowing recipient institutions to deliver courses in subjects where they lacked resources. The Sona institutions were among the early pioneers in digital learning. They offered a wide range of programmes ranging from skill-oriented computer-based technology (CBT) packages for school dropouts to advanced engineering subjects like graphics, design, textiles and quality. Additionally, they developed Tamil language learning programmes for the youth in twelve countries where Tamil is widely spoken or taught, including three nations where it is an official language.

Of course, the COVID-19 pandemic and the remote learning imperative ensured that all institutions had this facility. But Sona College was way ahead of the curve on delivering e-learning. It was the first licensee of Blackboard for campus, a global ed-tech solution founded in the mid-1990s.

Meaningful Research

The faculty and students of Sona colleges are actively involved in research beyond the daily demand of academia, many of which make meaningful contributions to society. For example, Professor T. Padma, professor in the Department of Computer Applications at Sona College of Technology, led a research project on the impact of cyber harassment on the mental health of young women, commissioned by the National Commission for Women, which collected data in 2018. The study, which surveyed 1,000 young women – about 800 in rural areas and the rest in cities – found that 175 of them had experienced cyber harassment. The college promptly launched an initiative to address cyberbullying.

Another example is Dr R. Malathy, head of Department of Civil Engineering, Sona College of Technology, who successfully completed five technology projects with strong sustainability quotient – paver block-making using steel slag, solar-powered vegetable dryer, pulse plating of silver anklets, waste paper recycling, special purpose sewing machines for women with lower limbs disabilities – under the Women's Technology Park (WTP) initiative to train and empower several hundred women to become independent.

The Sona Story

The project, which received a grant of ₹1.26 crore from the Technology Development Programme of the Department of Science and Technology, Government of India, in 2017, was recognised as a successful initiative in 2022. As a result of its impact, the project was awarded an additional grant, increasing the total funding to ₹2.77 crore.

The paver blocks project developed by the civil engineering department at Sona has found great applications. It was developed by mixing concrete with steel slag (the steel waste is collected from the Jindal Steel plant in the city). The technology was transferred to WTP, and rural women were trained to produce the blocks. The idea she says was to help the rural women set up their own pavement-tile-making units. The paver blocks are being used in the Sona campus and many other building projects. These valuable lessons have been captured in *Smart Villages*, a Springer publication, where Sona researchers have contributed two chapters.

In the summer of 2024, Stephen Ibaraki, a renowned technology futurist and global thought leader in AI, cybersecurity and digital transformation, interacted with the leadership, faculty and students at the Sona campus. He stated, 'It has been such a remarkable experience witnessing the outstanding, world-class innovation – the best I've seen in my entire career. Every aspect of the innovation that's occurring, the inviting environment for the students to co-create with other students, the faculty immersed in innovation are working hand in hand to create the most impactful technology in the world.' Ibaraki, recognised as Microsoft's Most Valuable Professional twenty-two times, emphasised, 'It's the highest concentration of talent I have seen in my lifetime. My interactions with students and faculty at the Sona institutions is a highlight of my life.'

8

Scaling Up and Making an Impact

In 2004, Valliappa's mother, Meenakshi, passed away and major differences surfaced between his brother and him. While Valliappa wanted to maintain the original social responsibility ethos of the college, his brother Sundaram didn't warm up to the idea. With two power centres, and Dhiraj Lal impeding the functioning of the college every now and then, Valliappa found it increasingly difficult to run the institution. Until he decided to settle with his brother. By 2006, through negotiations facilitated by his uncle Karumuttu Kannan, Valliappa successfully gained full control of the college.

But there remained Lal, who was proving quite a thorn in implementing the ideas the Valliappas had. By 2011, Lal's college had been established. Valliappa himself went to inaugurate it and wished the project luck. Dhiraj Lal, however, overreached himself by appointing another principal of the college without informing the Valliappas, and gave him all the powers, undermining the existing power. 'Imagine a situation where there are two principals in a college,' exclaims Chocko. The faculty was utterly confused. At this point, the Valliappas decided to ask Lal to leave. Freed of the presence of all the people who were curbing the expansion ideas of the group, Valliappa got a new burst of inspiration and motivation. Since then, there has been no looking back.

He roped in his trusted adviser Professor Kumar to help with the principal selection. Professor Kumar did a rigorous job, doing all the candidate interviews. Under his mentorship and guidance, the college blossomed, says Valliappa. At the first graduation speech of the college, he had asked Kumar for help with his speech. 'He told me to focus on the need for research,' says Valliappa. The college had earned thirty-eight patents by then.

The first round of principal selection did not yield a suitable candidate, but the Valliappas persevered. They eventually recruited S.R.R. Senthilkumar. 'We recalibrated the management and that is where the big growth of the campus started,' says Thyagu. Several new branches of computer science and engineering were introduced at the undergraduate and postgraduate level.

The Syllabus Grows

Sona College of Arts and Science was established in 2017 under the captainship of Dr G.M. Kadhar Nawaz, the head of the computer applications department at Sona College of Technology. He was entrusted with the responsibility of launching the new institution. When the idea was first proposed, members of Sona College of Technology and Thiagarajar Polytechnic College expressed concern that an arts and science college might compromise campus discipline. However, Valliappa, who had a forward-thinking vision and was conscious of the gaps in education delivery, was insistent. He established Sona College of Arts and Science in the middle of the academic year with three departments and just thirty-six students. This college was affiliated to Periyar University, Salem.

Kadhar Nawaz was initially hesitant about starting college mid-year, but Valliappa was confident about his decision.

Majestic opulence – The Darbar hall at Lakshmi Vilas in Poolankurichi, restored by architect Vikram Ponappa

Photo courtesy Vikram Ponappa

Aerial perspective – A bird's eye view of Poolankurichi Village, 2024

Traditional flooring – The veranda at Lakshmi Vilas, the Chettinad mansion of the Valliappas, restored to its former glory

The inspiration – Kalaithanthi Karumuttu Thiagarajar Chettiar

Valliappa's parents – Meenakshi Aachi and M.S. Chockalingam

A strong knot – Valliappa and Seetha Aachi's wedding was in true Chettinad style

At leisure – Valliappa and Seetha Aachi relaxing in a garden

Moonlight sonata – Valliappa at the Taj Mahal with Seetha Aachi

Tutelary deity – A view of Pillayarpatti temple

Revered figures – Pictures of Valliappa's parents with the beloved Vinayagar idol from Pillayarpatti temple

Back to the roots – At Poolankurichi, where a kalasa abhishekam marked the eightieth birthday celebrations (sadabhishekam)

Receiving blessings – At the sadabhishekam function

Bouquets and best wishes – Karnataka leader Basavaraj Bommai (*right*) greeting Seetha Aachi and Valliappa on Valliappa's eightieth birthday

Staying true to the roots – (*From left to right*) Chocko, Valliappa and Thyagu at Poolankurichi

Photo by J. Senthil Kumar

Stately at eighty – Valliappa decked in ceremonial finery during his sadabhishekam celebrations in Bengaluru

Scan the QR code to see more photographs
from the Valliappa gallery

Within six months, the college gained recognition across the state. The following academic year, all seats were filled on the first day of admissions. Every subsequent year, under Valliappa's leadership, new courses were added. The college now offers nineteen undergraduate and four postgraduate courses, including in commerce streams, though commerce does not figure in its name.

The motto of Sona Arts and Science college is 'Enabling Dreams Empowering Vision'. The college has lived up to this motto by consistently producing students who secure first-class honours in every discipline.In just seven years from 2017 to 2024, the college expanded impressively – from 36 students to 3500 – and bagged many awards year after year.

The college encourages students to hone their speaking skills through a Speakers' Forum both in English (Power Talk) and in Tamil (Pesalam vaanga) and insists they spend at least half an hour a day reading to keep abreast of the various styles of writing and new vocabulary.

Valliappa emphasises the importance of faculty development, ensuring their skills align with industry standards.

New Horizons

In 2022, the Sona College of Technology moved to a new, swank, state-of-the-art ten-storey building that would be the pride of any town. At 147 feet, it is the tallest building in Salem. In a way the building reflects Valliappa's sense of ambition and optimism. It was his dream to make the Sona College of Technology a deemed university and he decided to give it a constructive turn by setting up the university block.

This building is the dream project of Valliappa, who has had a say in the selection of every brick, slab and design, passionately interested in architecture as he is. The architects on the project were astounded to hear that Valliappa had no background in structural engineering, for he would often come up with a solution that the structural engineers on the team had not thought of.

The classrooms are spacious with massive windows to provide natural air circulation and light. For students of Civil and Structural Engineering the building is a noteworthy point of study as it uses different construction materials in concrete such as flat slab, low beam slab and deck slab, and a variety of flooring such as rough, natural stone, granite, wooden, vitrified tiles, Kota stone and more.

The 100,000 square foot building is a hub of collaboration, research and training and placements. It is symbolic of the futuristic thinking of the group, which has been bringing quality education to the doorstep of students from tier-2 and -3 towns and trying to reduce the hiring gap that exists when it comes to aspirational jobs.

The centrepiece of the Sona campus today is a new library, an inviting space designed like the massive public libraries in the US. The library building's inspiration comes from Valliappa's grandson Valli, as mentioned earlier. Abundant light and comfortable seating create a perfect ambiance for students to spend time in the library.

Adjacent to the library is an auditorium that can accommodate over 1,200 students in theatre-style seating, a 500-seat open-air theatre, a large training centre and seminar rooms for students, conference facility for faculty and an administrative block.

The way the space for the auditorium was carved is a measure of Valliappa's ingenuity. The architects had designed the space for two seminar halls. But Valliappa suggested that it be turned into an auditorium, as such an events space was necessary in a college. The architects raised many objections saying it was not possible to carve a stage, and a large hall would require pillars. In his trademark fashion, Valliappa listened quietly, before making a gentle suggestion. The RCC (reinforced concrete wall) was broken down, and designed as a beam, a place made for a stage and a semicircular room emerged, that could be accessed from outside as well as through the building.

Designed by IMK Architects, the campus features unique landscaping with sixty-two different varieties of plants, nearly 1,000 birds and a large water fountain that enhances the aesthetics while cooling the area. Rahul Kadri describes how Valliappa never imposed his ideas on the team, but through gentle suggestions nudged the architects to do what he wanted. Valliappa is particular about ensuring that every classroom and lab faces either north or south, with a corridor on the south side. Additionally, he mandates that no corridor should have classrooms or labs on both sides. This design keeps room temperatures lower and ensures that students are never more than 20 feet away from greenery. The hostel rooms face both east and west, allowing for maximum sunlight in the mornings and afternoons, respectively. This orientation allows for optimum use of natural light and temperature control, aligning with both traditional beliefs and modern energy efficiency practices, leading to a healthy living experience.

Recognising the importance of online education, the institution has made investments in a Sona YouTube channel, which has a sizeable number of videos and student subscribers.

The Sona campus operates with 600 faculty that includes 262 doctorates and 129 faculty members pursuing PhD Faculty members attest to the exceptional working environment at the institution. Valliappa is insistent on faculty being reskilled constantly and spends a lot on it. The faculty's performance has ranked No. 1 five times out of 6,000 engineering colleges on the National Programme on Technology Enhanced Learning (NPTEL) platform. NPTEL, an initiative by seven

Indian Institutes of Technology (IIT Bombay, IIT Delhi, IIT Guwahati, IIT Kanpur, IIT Kharagpur, IIT Madras and IIT Roorkee) and the Indian Institute of Science (IISc), is designed to create high-quality course content in engineering and science. The faculty at the college also command a high H-Index (a measure of productivity of researchers based on how many times their paper is cited). The faculty has over 650 research articles and 2,700 published papers.

The college has also received recognition for its excellent teacher–student ratio of 1:15, which promotes personalised learning alongside cutting-edge technological education. In 2024, Sona College was awarded NAAC A++ grade with a CGPA of 3.65, placing it among the premier educational institutions in India. The college aims to become a deemed university in the near future. With women being two in every five faculty and researchers and four in every ten students at the group's colleges, the Sona College of Technology was the indisputable winner of two national awards: the AICTE's Lilavati Awards 2020 for women entrepreneurship and for women's hygiene and sanitation. The 'Radiant Seetha' team from the group's Thiagarajar Polytechnic College, the first institution set up by the group, also won the contest in the 'legal awareness' category.

Clean and Green

Despite the new buildings that have come up on the 47-acre campus, it remains green and vibrant. The campus has plants such as the Nagalingapoo or the cannon ball flower, a revered flower in Tamil Nadu. The flower holds special significance in Hinduism, particularly in the worship of Lord Shiva, and is also called 'Siva Kundalam' because its shape resembles the earrings worn by the god.

Always abreast of the latest in the architectural field, Valliappa has directed the college to incorporate green features with innovative energy and water efficiency measures. These were put in place in the new Sona Sigma Block, the green building, where MCA and Mechatronics classes are held. Recycled water from the campus is used to water the plants and lawns.

The Sona Sigma block has earned the prestigious Green Rating for Integrated Habitat Assessment (GRIHA) 5-Star rating from The Energy Resources Institute (TERI). India's TERI GRIHA and the US Green Building Council's LEED Platinum ratings promote sustainable building practices. Valliappa's commitment to maintaining a clean and green campus has been recognised with an appreciation award from the AICTE for having a Clean and Smart Campus. Additionally, the campus has made significant contributions to the Jal Shakti Abhiyan, a national initiative aimed at water conservation. Just as Karumuttu Thiagarajar Chettiar was revered as 'Kalaithanthi' for his significant contribution to education and arts, his grandson Valliappa is fondly referred to as the Education Evangelist for his exemplary contribution to education.

Expanding Dreams

Having become self-reliant and progressive in offering higher education, the Sona Group decided to polish the uncut diamonds – children – with its new venture, the Sona Valliappa Public School in 2020.

By then Thyagu had begun implementing his ideas as well. Within the Sona campus is the Sona Ayush clinic which looks after the well-being of the community, offering yoga and pranayama. It was started during the COVID-19 pandemic. As Thyagu explains, 'Most programmes in the Sona institutions start with pranayama as we believe breathing is very important to beat stress.' In 2006, the Sona campus would had 3,000 students in all. In 2024, there were over 12,000 students.

Valliappa wants to get Sona College a deemed university status in the near future. Valliappa has acquired more land parcels to set up more institutions. He bid for a 50-acre land parcel located on the Salem–Kanyakumari National Highway 44. Although the deal would have tried the patience of any man, as there were too many suitors and obstacles, Valliappa bided his time patiently. Plans are afoot for a Sona Hospital, which will expand by offering nursing, paramedical training, and then a medical college.

When Valliappa thought of the medical college, he reached out to Dr K. Arthanari, the founder of Gokulam Hospitals in Salem, who was enthusiastic. Arthanari says that typically those with land and money venture into commercial businesses. But Valliappa has chosen to prioritise education. It is heartening to see him thinking of putting up something that will benefit the community. He believes Valliappa is a man of simplicity and intelligence.

For Valliappa, education is not complete without inculcating moral values and ethics. With this in mind he directed the colleges to organise regular motivational speeches by renowned spiritual persons. Among others there have been visits to the campus by Swamy Sri Sri Jayendra Puri of the Raja Rajeshwari temple in Bengaluru, who motivates the students regularly. Every last Saturday of the month he speaks to the students and faculty for an hour. Speakers like Suki Sivam and Parveen Sultana also regularly visit the campus.

The teachers at the Sona College of Arts and Science consider the campus a 'Punya Bhoomi' (blessed place). It's lucky for several people. 'People who come to write their CA exams at the Sona campus [it is an exam centre] usually do very well. In fact, two students who wrote the exams here topped all-India rankings, bagging the first rank twice – a unique distinction for a town like Salem,' says Chocko.

People on the campus underscore how invested Valliappa is in the success and happiness of the college. When he stays in the family quarters on campus, he insists on using the same furniture and bed as the students, as well as on eating the same food. 'The idea is to personally check out the standards being served to the students,' says Adhiyaman.

Almost a hundred years after the Madurai episode, the Sona college still strives to preserve Gandhian values at the campus. On International Women's Day in 2011, Gandhiji's granddaughter Sumitra Gandhi Kulkarni visited the campus along with her husband, Professor Gajanan Kulkarni. While addressing the students, she reminisced about her time with Mahatma Gandhi and spoke about the role of students in nation-building. She praised Valliappa's efforts in elevating the stature of the Sona institutions, its numerous achievements, and wished it global leadership soon.

Mr M. Kalyanam, personal secretary and close associate of Gandhiji and a freedom fighter, visited the campus for the community college graduation just before passing away in the 1960s and shared many anecdotes about the father of the nation. His message to the students: Take care of the nation.

9

Dharmam: The Art of Giving

THE SONA VALLIAPPA group has always believed in and practised philanthropy. As Valliappa often quotes, the Chettiar credo is 'Make profits but give back'.

If textile magnate Karumuttu Thiagarajar Chettiar, the visionary founder of the group, set up nineteen educational institutions in response to a call from nation builders for industrialists to support education, then his scions have expanded on his ideals.

When Valliappa was first sent to Bengaluru to manage the textile operations, the location was so remote that there were no schools for the children of the workers. In response, he immediately set up Chockalingam Vidyalaya, a school that continues to serve the local community even though the mill has since closed.

For the Chettiars, if creating wealth is in their genes, so is daanam or philanthropy. Alagu Alagappan, a friend of the Valliappa family and founder of Blossom Educational Institutions in Thanjavur, says that the tradition of giving has been going on since the beginning when the family's ancestors made their riches in Burma and returned to India.

Valliappa himself illustrates this philosophy with a story of a Chettiar lady in a Karaikudi village who was bargaining furiously with a vegetable seller, driving down the price of tomatoes and carrots. But after the hard bargaining, she asked the girl selling the vegetables if she had eaten, and then insisted on giving her a lavish meal. Her son, who was observing, asked her, 'Why did you bargain so much with her when you have given her a meal that costs more than what you saved?' To which the lady replied, 'I bargain to get the right value. And I feed her because I should help her.'

Valliappa says, 'It is exactly like that in my book. One is Vyaparam, where one must ensure fairness. The other is Dharmam, where one should always help the needy.'

Sometimes, Valliappa says, the Chettiars can take philanthropy too far, especially if they have made a promise. He narrates the story of Dr Alagappa Chettiar, the great philanthropist. His mills and his educational institutions were in crisis and Kalaithanthi Karumuttu Chettiar, who had great regard for him, stepped in to help. In 1950, when Alagappa Chettiar fell seriously ill in Chennai and had lost everything, Karumuttu anonymously left a packet containing ₹10,000 at his bedside. Remarkably, Alagappa Chettiar immediately donated the entire amount to the principal in need of funds for a school building. 'When a Chettiar makes a promise, it is always kept,' says Valliappa.

Valliappa contributed liberally for the construction of the Nagarathar Sangam building in Bengaluru. The Nagarathars have set up 139 of these Sangams in India, Malaysia, Norway, Singapore, UAE, UK and USA.

Valliappa's associates say he is like the proverbial Chettiar who drives a hard bargain in business and loves to negotiate, but is lavishly generous when it comes to his pet charities, mostly educational causes and temples. 'Chairman Sir has given away nearly five crore rupees of fee waiver from his personal kitty to help needy students at Sona College of Technology,' says a teacher.

Valliappa, who often sits in on student interviews, explains, 'Banks are often reluctant to give loans to students. I feel because of want students should not suffer. So I started an interest-free loan scheme where I lend them for the course, on a returnable basis.'

In 2023, when a set of triplets from Thanjavur town applied for admission to the Sona College of Technology in Salem, Valliappa's curiosity was piqued. He wanted to meet them. The siblings – Dhanushree, Dhanush and Dhanuja – stood out as the two girls opted for Mechanical Engineering, a rare choice for women, while their brother opted for electronic engineering.

Their academic excellence was remarkable, and while securing admission was easy, the hostel fees for all three were a burden for their parents. Kamala, their mother, a state government employee, and Murugan, their father, a business owner, approached Valliappa for concessional hostel fees. Valliappa jokingly suggested they relocate to Salem to make the expenses more manageable. To his surprise, the family agreed, and the college extended full support to the siblings.

For the Sona Group, philanthropy and corporate social responsibility (CSR) activities are institutionalised through the Valliappa foundation. Through the Foundation, it has helped the communities in the places it operates – especially in focusing on skill development and encouraging entrepreneurship.

Through the foundation scholarships are awarded at the Sona College of Technology to over a hundred students of BTech programmes under various categories, such as the physically challenged, whose parents' income is below ₹2 lakh per year, wards of deceased and serving defence personnel, ex-servicemen and based on performance in the extracurricular activities of the National Service Scheme (NSS), the National Cadet Corps (NCC), Youth Red Cross and Red Ribbon Club.

Working through Partnerships

Valliappa's belief is that initiatives work best through partnerships. Thus, the Valliappa Foundation has partnered with

Tech Mahindra Foundation and through the Skills for Market Training Program (SMART) has trained 5,000 underprivileged young girls in Chennai and Hyderabad in medical coding. In addition to training them, the foundation has also placed these students in various jobs. Many of them have been hired by Sona Group company Vee Technologies for its IT services business for the global healthcare sector.

Another CSR partner for the Valliappa Foundation is the German industry major Bosch. Together with the Bosch–Bridge programme, which aims at employability enhancement, the Foundation provides skill-based training in areas such as Information Technology and Information Technology Enabled Services (ITES), automobile, retail, hospitality, banking and electronics.

When the National Skills Development Corporation called upon corporates and educational institutes to aid in teaching vocational skills to the youth, the Sona Group stepped up by creating a skilling arm, Sona Yukti, to partner with the government in providing opportunities for the disadvantaged. It set up sixteen vocational schools in rural India.

However, as Valliappa says, it is not enough to skill people. The loop had to be closed. It was imperative to ensure that once people were skilled, they were employable. Thus was born the job matchmaking platform HireMee, the Sona Group's CSR programme, which assesses graduating students on general key skills and specific subject knowledge that help employers identify the most suitable candidates. HireMee tries to bridge the gap between recruiters and fresh graduates, especially in tier-2 and -3 towns. Launched in 2017, more than 750,000 students had completed the free assessments by 2024, and out of that 280,000 received opportunities from employers. Almost 72 per cent were from tier-2 and -3 towns and 37 per cent were women.

The impact of the Sona Group's CSR efforts is visible throughout Salem. At the WTP run by the Sona College of Technology, there is a strong focus on empowering women entrepreneurs. Using a grant of ₹2.77 crore from the Department of Science and Technology, the WTP has trained 700 women. One of the notable successes includes a woman who established a pavement tile-making unit.

A key innovation at the WTP is the modification of industrial sewing machines to include sensor-based assistive technology, enabling individuals with lower limb disabilities to operate the machines using only their hands. The Fashion Technology faculty led by Professor D. Raja worked tirelessly with the WTP team to modify the industrial sewing machine with sensor-based assistive technology that could be operated solely by hand. As many as 150 women have been trained to operate these machines, empowering them to break free from their limitations and boost their self-esteem and support their families. One such participant shared her elation, 'I wear a special shoe, but after being introduced to the Sona College machine, I no longer feel I am different. I feel more confident than ever before and am happy that I can make a living for myself and my family.'

Another innovation at the WTP is the solar drying unit. Recognising the significant food waste in agricultural areas around Salem, the WTP developed this unit to help preserve produce. Similarly, there are innovations created for the silver anklet industry, which Salem is famous for. It introduced pulse plating technology instead of the usual DC coating, which reduced the health hazards faced by polishers during the traditional process.

In 2019, the AICTE mandated all accredited engineering colleges in the country to facilitate 400 hours of rural development community service during their 4-year programme, with credits awarded for the service. The Valliappa Foundation helped 1000 students at the BNMIT College of Engineering, Bengaluru, undertake this community service in five areas – Swachh Bharat and digital literacy, technical solutions, lake restoration, garbage disposal and traffic rules observance.

Stepping Up during COVID-19

The group contributed to society in multiple ways during the COVID-19 pandemic. Faculty and students at Sona College of Technology collaborated with the IT teams of Vee Technologies to create VeeTrace, an app to track, trace and protect the community in Salem, Erode, Dharmapuri and Krishnagiri districts of Tamil Nadu. The Valliappa family invested time in encouraging their faculty as well as students to innovate and respond to pandemic. Scores of requests from the community for help with medical equipment, medicines, etc., were met swiftly and with empathy.

For the group's employees Valliappa ensured that Corona Kavach insurance cover was secured with speed bringing financial relief to many affected by the deadly virus. Valliappa and his wife were the first ones to receive the COVID-19 vaccine to encourage the hesitant employees and their families to get vaccinated.

The Valliappa Foundation donated lakhs of masks to the chief minister of Karnataka and to frontline workers in the Dharmapuri, Krishnagiri and Sivagangai districts as well as to civic bodies and police to distribute to the community. Tens of thousands of packets of dry ration were distributed to the migrant labour and those out of jobs due to the shutdown in and around Salem.

Valliappa says it was amazing how Salem's leading industries rallied together during the pandemic. Sona Group's employees had contributed a day's salary. 'The management contributed a week's salary,' he says.

Through collaborations, a temporary 500-bed COVID Care hospital was set up quickly at the Salem Steel Plant. The cafeteria at Sona College of Technology, which was closed due to closure of educational institutions, was converted into a community kitchen serving hot meals to the COVID-19 patients and poor and needy.

One challenge during this period was managing the supply and demand for meals and ensuring no food went to waste. This was managed through Anadhanam.org, a digital platform created by Vee Tech. Says Chocko, 'The platform has applications beyond COVID, as it streamlines the donation and distribution process.'

With India-wide lockdown announced on 24 March 2020, the labour working on construction projects was stranded. The workers were sheltered at the Sona Education group campus. They were provided hot meals and essentials. All this was done while maintaining strict guidelines of social distancing, hand washing and use of masks.

As soon as the COVID-19 pandemic outbreak was declared, Valliappa Foundation made timely efforts to serve the society by donating groceries, including rice and pulses. The foundation also donated sanitizers, two-layered fabric reusable masks and nitrile gloves.

The COVID-19 period was tough for families all over as many lost their jobs and those who had businesses of their own suffered huge losses. The Sona Group employees say this was the period when they were most grateful to be a part of the company. Says Anuradha Rameshbabu, who heads the English department at the Sona College of Arts and Science, 'Our family has three businesses. They halted during the pandemic, and it was my salary that tided the household during the time.

We were hearing from teachers in other colleges about salary cuts, but we were fortunate to get our full salaries all through the pandemic.'

She added that the staff at Sona feel emotionally attached to the institute because of the warm and family-like atmosphere and treatment by the chairman. 'Sona is in our blood. Many of us regard this as our punya bhoomi as good things tend to happen here. Newly joined staff members will find their marriages getting solemnised. Many have become parents.'

The Valliappa Foundation has also adopted villages, with the idea of transforming them into Smart Villages. This includes interventions that would lead to economic development, infrastructure development and other aspects of human development, such as education, health and drinking water supply.

Apart from the work done through the Valliappa Foundation, the Sona Group chairman and his family have done yeomen charity for several causes. Seetha Aachi, as Inner Wheel president, worked to better a village near Bengaluru called Thavarakarai. The Rotary club had adopted the village and built a school there and during her tenure she doanted furniture. 'We also worked on improving nutrition of the children,' she says.

More to Giving than Cash

Valliappa believes there is more to giving than cash. He is the person people turn to when in crisis. When Edward White, from whom he bought the coffee estate in Chikkamagaluru, called up saying his mother was critically ill, it was Valliappa who helped by suggesting he take a second opinion from Dr Stanley John. The referral increased her lifespan by ten years, believes White.

He describes how his sister was in France and his brother in England, when his mother had a heart attack. She was rushed to a hospital and seen by all the surgeons, who opined that it was too dangerous to do the surgery. At this point, Valliappa recommended they should see Dr John, who said it was safe to do the surgery. 'He saved my mother's life,' says White.

Similarly, Valliappa was there at hand even when his estranged brother Sundaram fell ill and was hospitalised, and none of his children could be with him. Later, when his brother died, it was Valliappa who stepped in and made all arrangements for a grand funeral.

It's hard to list all the charitable actions that Valliappa has done. A marriage hall in Bengaluru, donations to scores of temples, there is no count of how much Valliappa has given.

In his village Poolankurichi, the Anjaneya temple has been completely restored by Valliappa. At the Pillayarpatti temple in Chettinad, which is the family's ruling deity, Valliappa donated a golden armour for the deity.

During the consecration of a Hanuman temple in Salem, Valliappa offered help. The temple in charge requested 1,000 food packets for the devotees. Without hesitation, Valliappa generously sanctioned 2,500 food packets. As it happened, around 2,400 devotees attended, and all the food was consumed, showing his foresight.

He also showed foresight when a big event – the unique wedding ceremony of Tirupati Balaji – was held in Sona College. Valliappa commissioned ten restrooms on the grounds for devotees to use, showing his practical nature.

Says P. Muralidhar, COO of Vee Technologies, 'The Chairman is a little more generous than what he could be, but then he loves to do it. It's not just he wants to do it. He takes a lot of pride in doing some of those things through the Valliappa Foundation, through the family trust, through the college and whenever and wherever he gets an opportunity, he will do. All that culture has come into the companies too.'

For instance, he says, 'During the 2018 Karnataka flood, almost all the employees on their own contributed, either in food or in cash.' Nobody forced it, nobody told them to do that but then the culture is the sort that cascades down the levels and they were happy doing it. The employees brought clothes from their homes, and a few brought groceries and snacks and distributed these. During the COVID-19 pandemic, everybody agreed to contribute one-day salary and Chocko doubled that and contributed to Prime Minister CARES Fund.

10

The Divine Connection: Faith and Spirituality

THEY SAY YOU can take a Chettiar out of Chettinad but you cannot take Chettinad out of the Chettiar. Extremely God-fearing and rooted in tradition, the Valliappas continue to staunchly uphold all the values of the community. Most Chettiars are big donors to temples. They also take their daily prayers seriously. And while they celebrate the big festivals of Pongal and Diwali, some festivals, such as the festival of risk, are unique to their community.

Pointing out the Chettiars' long history of association with some of the biggest temples in India, Valliappa says, 'At the Kashi Vishwanath temple in Varanasi, the items for abhishekam – sambho – is supplied by our community three times a day. They have been giving it for over one hundred and sixty years through the Sri Kashi Nattukottai Nagarthar Satram.'

Likewise, the Meenakshi Amman Temple, Madurai has received generous contributions from the Chettiars. In the 1940s, the Nagarathars donated ₹25 lakh for the construction of the temple. Their generosity extended to building the Kambathadi Mandapam and the north Gopuram. According to the records, the Amaravathiputhur Vayanagaram family contributed the funds.

Valliappa says that most Nagarathars have spent a large amount of money from their business profits on religious works. In the olden days, they would collect money every evening

The Divine Connection: Faith and Spirituality

from each firm for building temples. They did this not just in India but also in the foreign shores where they established their businesses. Nagarathars were the prime movers behind many of the Murugan temples across Asia.

Following the community practice, Valliappa also made several donations and has helped in reviving many temples. One of the first temples Valliappa's family was a patron to was the Murugan temple, Dhwaralingam or Vallilingam. Almost everyone in this village bears one or the other name of Lord Murugan. Valliappa's name too is one of these. The boys in the families were named Valliappa and the girls were named Valliammai.

Reminiscing about the historical events that shaped the culture of the Nagarathars, Valliappa says, in the days of yore, there were thousands of mansions in the seventy-six villages that made up the Chettinad region, which straddled the arid Pudukkottai and Sivaganga districts. Karaikudi, an educational centre, forms the Chettinad heartland. The Chettiars of these villages are affiliated to nine clan temples, which have been described in an earlier chapter.

People who belong to the same temple or village call one another 'Kovil Pangaligal' or 'Oor Pangaligal' and when they meet each other away from home, the fact that they hail from the same place serves as a strong binding factor.

The ancient Pillayarpatti temple situated between Karaikudi and Pudukkottai is the lineage deity of the entire Nagarathar community and they have been the patrons for long. This is the only temple in Tamil Nadu which has a six-foot rock-cut idol of Lord Pillayar, another name for Lord Ganesha. The trunk (thumbikai) of Lord Pillayar is curled towards his right side, which is a unique feature and so the god is known as Valampuri Pillayar. Also, here you will find Lord Ganesha holding a shivalingam in his hands. This is a rare temple where the idol has two hands – mostly the lord is depicted with four hands.

The Sona Story

According to local legends, there is a reason why Lord Ganesha's idol has been hewn out of a rock. In the old days, when warring kings attacked each other's territories, the winner would loot and take away all the idols in the area. To prevent this, the people of the region decided to carve the idol out of a rock.

Valliappa follows Shaivism, like everyone in the Nagarathar community. Traditionally, the Nagarathars belong to the Shaivite branch of Hinduism whose clan temples are all dedicated to Lord Shiva. Fifteen centuries ago, when the Nagarathars lived in Kaveripoompattinam, they worshipped Maragatha Vinayagar (emerald Vinayagar idol), believed to now be with a branch of Nagarathars settled down in the Nagercoil area. Chettiars are the only community whose subcastes are divided based on Shiva temples.

The governance of the Pillayarpatti temple moves every year by rotation among the twenty families attached to the temple with each family getting its chance once in eight years. The rule is that one person from the family has to stay in the temple. When Valliappa's family was in-charge (thakkar) of the temple of Pillayarpatti in 2016, they had two rajagopurams (royal towers) renovated. They also donated a thangakavasam (golden armour) to the Karpaga Vinayagar.

'My father has a deep appreciation for the intersection of tradition and science, particularly within the context of temple culture. He is driving research on oil and wicks to find alternatives to traditional lamp lighting in temples, as smoke from the oil lamps tarnishes the beauty of the intricate carvings on the pillars and walls of these ancient architectural wonders. This reflects his thoughtful approach to preserving temple heritage,' says Thyagu.

In 2023, the management of the Pillayarpatti again came to the Valliappa family, a responsibility taken very seriously

The Divine Connection: Faith and Spirituality

by them and a matter of great pride. Under their watch, one crore archanas or offerings were made continuously for four months to the presiding deity – Lord Ganesha. The Valliappas also presented a golden ornament to adorn the deity.

There are other temples too where Valliappa plays a key role. In Salem, the Government of Tamil Nadu appointed Valliappa as the chairman of the trust boards of three main temples – Rajaganapathi temple, Arulmigu Sugavaneswara temple and Arulmigu Kasiviswanathar temple – a responsibility he takes very seriously.

He says that at the Rajaganapathi temple, there was no sutruprakaram room and it was his father who enabled its construction. At the Sugavaneswara temple, Valliappa took the responsibility of dredging the temple pond (kolam) by scooping out mud, weeds and rubbish. The kumbhabhishekam of the Sugavaneswara temple had been delayed a long time. When Valliappa took charge, he at once ensured that the long-delayed consecration ceremony that is supposed to harmonise, synergise and unite the mystic powers of the deity was held.

Like his grandfather, Valliappa is a passionate pilgrim. Whenever he finds time, he undertakes pilgrimage to different temples. In Bengaluru, he is a frequent visitor to the Sri Rajarajeswari temple, and he reads the holy hymns sung by the great Tamil saints before visiting the temple.

It is a tradition at the Valliappa home to pass down stories of gods and spiritual tales from generation to generation. And what tales these are! While some are common stories – the Ramayana and the Mahabharata – from across India, the Nagarathars have their own unique tales.

Valliappa grew up listening to his elders' stories about temples and the power of faith. From his grandfather and mother he also imbibed a love for Thiruvasagam and Thevaram hymns, sacred utterances that are full of divine love. He describes how his mother, Meenakshi Aachi would play the harmonium and chant sholkas in her daily prayers. 'She prayed to God with complete renouncement and total bhakti,' he says.

Even today, he says, on his grandfather's birth and death anniversaries, the faculty members at the college sing the Thevaram and Thiruvasagam hymns.

Karumuttu loved to narrate stories connected with various temples, such as the one about the temple at Thiruppuvanam in Sivaganga district, celebrated by the three great saints Appar, Sundarar and Gnanasambandar. The temple has been established at one of the sixty-four places where Lord Shiva is said to have performed his Thiruvilayadal or divine play.

Ponnanaiyal, a dancing girl and an ardent devotee of Lord Shiva, longed to make a gold idol of him but she did not have the means to do so. The Lord appeared before her as a Siddha and bade her to bring all the iron, copper, lead and brass vessels with her and converted them into gold. An ecstatic Ponnanaiyal then fashioned a beautiful golden idol of Lord Shiva. So pleased was she with her creation that she lovingly pinched its cheeks and the mark is visible on the idol even today.

Valliappa believes that he owes his success and prosperity to Lord Shiva. He recalls how his grandfather Karumuttu insisted that theological colleges and schools for teaching Saiva Siddhanta and the Tirumurais should be established throughout the land. As long as Avvai S. Duraisamy Pillai was on the rolls, Saiva Siddhanta classes were conducted regularly in Thiagarajar College. Karumuttu also had an idea of starting a Saiva Siddhanta research centre in the college. His wish was fulfilled by his grandson in 1981.

The Divine Connection: Faith and Spirituality

Valliappa has many stories to share on divine interventions. He describes how at the Meenakshi Amman temple in Madurai, where his uncle Karumuttu Kannan was trustee, there was a big debate on the date of the kumbhabhishekam. Two dates were shortlisted, and they decided to draw lots before the deity. On two chits of paper, the dates were written, and after the aarati, a young girl in the crowd was asked to come forward and pick up the chit. His uncle asked the girl her name and when she replied Meenakshi, the entire crowd gasped.

On another occasion he was present at the Rajaganapathi temple when they were opening the hundi (the donation box in which devotees put their coins and rupee notes). A few students from TPT were assigned to count. While they were counting, they noticed a piece of paper in the hundi, which they simply set aside. Curious, Valliappa picked it up and discovered the newspaper clipping highlighting the placement details of TPT.

Festival of Risk

Pillayar Nonbu is a unique and important festival for the Chettiars, which Valliappa's family celebrates with great fervour every year, and it involves eating fire. It is celebrated once a year in December–January, on the twenty-first day after Thiru Karthikai or Periya Karthikai, as it is called.

Lord Ganesha is worshipped by observing a fast for twenty-one days, beginning from the Thiru Karthikai day. On these days, only one square meal (palagaram) is taken.

The origins of the festival are fascinating. Says Valliappa, 'Hundreds of years ago our forefathers set sail to the Far East to set up merchant banking enterprises. They were marooned en route and prayed to Lord Ganesha and kept count of days by taking strands of thread. Finally on the twenty-first day they were rescued.'

Even today, the community celebrates the spirit of enterprise by praying to Pillayar, lighting a wick with twenty-one strands of thread and eat fire with a sweet base — symbolising no risk no reward. The Nagarathar Association (of which Valliappa was the president for sixteen years) organises Pillayar Nonbu in Bengaluru in a grand way and over a thousand people attend to swallow fire. It is also organised in cities having a significant population of Chettiars.

The twenty-first day, the last day of the Nonbu, is the day when Sashti converges with Sathya Nakshatram. It is a day of total fasting and the regular meal recommences after the final prayer is offered to Pillayar. During these twenty-one days, a thread from a new veshti/dhothi is drawn and kept before the god. On the twenty-first day, all these twenty-one threads are collected and twisted together to make the wicks needed for the function. On the day of the Nonbu, a special Pillayar is placed on the Nadu Veetu Kolam (a special kolam which is used only for auspicious occasions) in the pooja room together with a bunch of auspicious flowers (avvarampoo), tied around a small stick. The Pillayar is beautifully decorated with flowers and garlands. The prasadams are placed before the god.

The delicacy offered as prasadam to the lord is Karupatti Panniyaram. Twenty-one threads, dipped in ghee, are kept in the centre of the pyramid. Other dishes which are offered to the lord are vellai panniyaram made using rice flour, ulunduvadai and thirattupaal made from milk. In addition, there are offerings such as puffed sesame seeds, puffed rice, puffed maize, puffed millet, kadalai (peanuts) urundai, ellu urundai, fruits, betel leaves and paaku (nuts).

The panniyaram dough is also used to create small pyramid-shaped Ganeshas. At the end of the pooja, they swallow the lighted camphor placed on the jaggery.

The Divine Connection: Faith and Spirituality

Spreading the Faith

Valliappa is very fond of inviting religious personalities and listening to their discourse. He follows the philosophy of 'Let the world avail of the bliss I attained' and ensures that others get the same pleasure of listening to spiritual discourses and organises these events at his educational institutes.

Among others, Mata Amritanandamayi has graced the college with her presence. Valliappa has also periodically organised Sri Srinivasa Thirukalyanam (the celestial wedding of Lord Venkateswara with Sridevi and Bhoomadevi) at the Sona College premises. It is a truly magnificent event touching the hearts of everyone who has attended. It is the only place outside of Tirupati where this celestial wedding has been organised four times.

Swami Sri Sri Jayendra Puri Mahaswamiji, of the Raja Rajeshwari temple in Bengaluru, says he is impressed by Valliappa's unswerving devotion and piety, noting how he has observed that Valiappa has never missed visiting the nagarathar mandagapidi (Simmavaganam) in forty years and how on the last day of Sri Rama Navami he visits Sri Raja Rajeshwari temple.

'He doesn't just stop at visiting the temples but volunteers in several activities,' says Swamiji.

It's the faith that perhaps explains Valliappa's calm attitude to life.

11

Love for Tamil

THE LOCKDOWN BROUGHT on by the COVID-19 pandemic was a strange period for everyone. Cooped indoors, and cut away from people, hobbies and hidden interests surfaced. People rediscovered their passions.

In Valliappa's case, it was his love for Tamil literature. He rediscovered the classic Tamil texts, read them with intellectual interest, almost like a student. He would call up the Tamil faculty in his college or experts and debate points about the texts. It was a deeply satisfying exploratory journey of the rich literary volumes in Tamil.

One's mother tongue is precious and one should always have mastery over it, believes Valliappa. Although he is not chauvinistic about the Tamil language and has embraced Kannada, Hindi and other languages, his love for his mother tongue — one of the oldest living languages in the world — led him to often dip into the classical texts and he can quote stories and classic poetry with ease.

He describes how his interest was whetted during his college days when he got to know that the Chettiars had a role to play in the propagation of the language.

For instance, the orator, writer and freedom fighter Chinna Annamalai established a press named Tamil Pannai. He published the works of Rajaji and the Namakkal poet Ramalingam Pillai. Later, after meeting Gandhiji, he started

Love for Tamil

publishing *Harijan* magazine in Tamil with permission from the Mahatma. Then there was the prodigious Tamil writer P.L. Muthiah, better known as Mullaipathipagam Muthiah, who printed the magazine *Mullai*.

Hearing about these tall leaders of the community and creative people in his college days, when he was a leader of the youth wing of Nagarathar Association leader, hugely inspiring for Valliappa.

But much before that the Tamil bug had bit him, when after school hours his grandfather Karumuttu would quiz him on Tamil literature. Karumuttu had learnt Saiva Siddhanta under Chitkailasa Pillai, a Tamil and Sanskrit scholar of great eminence. Pillai belonged to a family of traditional Tamil scholars at Nallur in Jaffna. He was the official poet of Thiruvavaduthurai Adheenam, a Saivite muth (famous for presenting the golden sceptre to Jawaharlal Nehru in 1947). Scholars such as C.V. Damodaran Pillai and Navalar Sababathy had been his students. He had translated Kalidasa's *Shakunthalam* into Tamil. He had taught Saivite philosophical works to the members of the Vivekananda Sabha, Colombo.

Karumuttu also studied *Tolkappiam*, Sangam works like *Pattupattu*, *Purananuru* and Kalladam Saiva Siddhanta and Thayumanavar's songs under Chitkailasa Pillai.

It was another Pillai, A. Varathananjaiya Pillai, who would instill the love of Tamil in Valliappa. He was his schoolteacher and narrated great Tamil stories to his class. A renowned scholar, Varathananjaiya Pillai had won many accolades for his teaching from the Karanthai Tamil Sangam and for his poetry.

Tamil lends itself to beautiful puns and the play of language enchanted Valliappa. He is fond of narrating a story full of wordplay. The story goes thus: A poet goes to the king's court and sings his praises. He does not stop and goes on eulogising the ruler. In appreciation of his recital, the king decides to reward him with gold coins. He states, 'Iru naan mun tharavendiya airamporkaa sugalaitharukeran (Wait, you will be rewarded with a thousand gold coins for your attempt).'

He then commands his attendants to bring in the reward. The obedient servant brings the coins and places them on a silver plate. The king calls upon the poet and asks him to accept the prize money (Kirtan keertahanai). The poet says there is an inappropriate calculation in the reward money. The king asks how. The poet makes him recall his statement: 'Iru (two hundred gold coins) naan (four hundred gold coins) mun (three hundred) tharavendiya airamporkaa sugalaitharukeran.'

He says adding up along with the thousand gold coins given as reward, it would be ten thousand gold coins.

The king was dumbstruck and without further delay he orders the attendants to bring him ten thousand gold coins immediately. When the king was about to reach the silver plate to take the reward, the poet, who seemed lost in his thoughts, asked the king if the silver plate (panathattu) belonged to the king or him. 'Panathattuhas' could mean a money plate or scarcity. Now the king became speechless and awed by the poet's wordplay and without a second thought gave him plate along with the reward of ten thousand gold coins.

During his college days, Valliappa nurtured his love for Tamil by striking connections with S.A.P. Annamalai of *Kumudam* magazine and the writer Kalki Krishnamoorthy.

At college, he was initially the student chairman of the Hindi Association. But then he began focusing more on Tamil, influenced by a few Tamil professors. One such was Professor C. Balasubramaniam, who later became the vice-chancellor of Thanjavur Tamil University.

Another great Tamil legend who later became a good friend was M. Varatharajan, who introduced him to P.V. Akilandam, a director at Madras radio station. He was the first Tamil to win the Jnanpith Award for his novel *Chitra Pavai*. Akilan gave Valliappa a chance to address the public twice. Valliappa grabbed the opportunity to talk about Thirukurral and textiles. In another incident, he had a chance to publish one of his articles in the Tamil *Nagarathar* journal.

Later, during his grandfather's holiday excursions to Kodaikanal, where he would be surrounded by a coterie of scholars and intellectuals, Valliappa had a chance to listen to many a stimulating discussion on the Tamil classics.

Shaped by these experiences, Valliappa insisted on having a Tamil Literary Club in all his institutions, including Sona College of Technology, which initially had no course in Tamil at all. At the Sona College of Arts, the Tamil faculty has been handpicked by him.

Every year, Valliappa also organises a grand event related to Tamil on International Mother Language day at the Sona Campus. On one occasion, the popular orator and television speaker Kalaimamani Suki Sivam was invited as one of the chief guests. Valliappa himself has made deeply emotional and personal speeches recalling all his experiences and encounters with Tamil literature.

12

Passion for Art and Architecture

AT THE LARGE, airy, window-lined office of Valliappa, a serious discussion was on. A vexing problem confronted the chairman, the principal of the Sona College of Technology, the group of architects, IMK Architects, and the civil engineering team at the campus. A new building was necessary for the many expansions planned for the college, but the site engineers had been unable to find any area in the 47-acre campus large enough to create another structure.

And then Valliappa came up with a clever suggestion – to create a narrow block between the new 10-storey building and the old college block. The architects were sceptical. They had been over the area and did not think it was big enough. Nevertheless, everyone went down to take a look. By relocating the trees and some of the underground cables, it was feasible to build here.

As the principal, Senthilkumar, points out, 'Our chairman is not a trained engineer or architect, and yet he can see things that qualified structural engineers and site engineers cannot.'

It was not the first time that Valliappa found solutions to an architectural problem. Passionate about buildings and architecture, he loved nothing better than to pore over drawings and plans and try to come up with better ways of executing them. And his ability to think out of the box would often help.

Passion for Art and Architecture

At the Sona College of Technology, one glaring gap was the lack of an auditorium. The architects had designed a space in the basement for two large seminar halls. Valliappa suggested that it be turned into an auditorium, as such an events space was necessary in a college. The architects raised many objections saying it was not possible to carve a stage in that space and that a large hall would require pillars.

In his trademark fashion, Valliappa listened quietly before making a gentle suggestion. The RCC (reinforced concrete wall) was broken down, and designed as a beam, a place was made for a stage and a semicircular room emerged, which could be accessed both from outside and from within the building. In addition, Valliappa suggested that the outdoor entrance area be designed like a small amphitheatre. This is now a truly brilliant space that the students use for rehearsals or small performances.

Another occasion where he surprised the institute's civil engineering team was when altering the roof of the Sona Varsity building – 600 square feet of the 1500 square foot roofing had got damaged. It was a heritage building and the original roofing material, semi-corrugated asbestos sheets, was no more in production. When M. Adhiyaman, the project engineer at Sona College of Technology, approached Valliappa, the chairman told him to divide the section into two and replace the worn parts with the intact sheets from the other side and replace the second part with a new roofing material available in the market – a simple suggestion that had not occurred to the team.

Says Adhiyaman, 'When a construction plan for a building or a laboratory is taken to the chairman, I have to make a feasible study and present him with ten plans. Each time, Mr Valliappa comes out with an eleventh idea which turns out to be brilliant and results in the final structure.'

After the success of Sona Towers built in the 1980s, Valliappa had always been keen to work on buildings, but other businesses had kept him busy. Then at the age of seventy-five he returned to his passion for architecture with the Sona Vistaas project off Bannerghatta Road in Bengaluru. With his favourite IMK Architects, he crafted an elegant, green, contemporary low-rise community living space with every conceivable amenity that a young couple working in Electronic City would want. From swank gymnasiums to pools to a club and banquet area, sports facilities and lovely seating spaces between apartment blocks so that neighbours could sit and chat with each other, it's a thoughtfully conceived project with Valliappa's distinctive stamp.

Indeed, all the buildings he constructed for his mills, IT companies, Sona FM Tower and educational institutions bear Valliappa's architectural philosophy.

Adhiyaman, who is a civil engineer by training and also teaches at Sona, says, 'One cannot make out if it is his keen eye or his interest which makes him pick out even a slight fault in a structure. He literally measures every inch of the building without any measurement tool. Besides, he applies complex civil engineering techniques to tackle issues related to structures and frameworks.'

Adhiyaman has numerous anecdotes about Valliappa's sharp thinking and engineering mind. He says that once Valliappa asked if there was any non-laser-based measurement tool to measure the height of a building from ground level and from top to bottom, apart from the regular tape measures. Adhiyaman told him there was no such instrument in the market. After much scouting, the team found a machine with a camera installed in it. When the camera machine was taken to Valliappa, he asked if the readings on the camera could be zoomed. He was enthusiastic about the machine and wanted to know if the readings on it should be transferred through Bluetooth or through wi-fi or a cable. The questions that he asked about the mechanics of the device surprised Adhiyaman.

Passion for Art and Architecture

But as Chocko says, buildings have always been an abiding passion for his father and it always manifested itself. 'Once when we were kids we had gone to Hong Kong on a family sightseeing trip. Suddenly we saw our father's attention riveted on a building being constructed that was fifty floors high. There was a cage-like lift which was taking workers up and down the building. My father wanted to go on that cage lift. Today of course security and safety is a concern and we would never have been allowed. But those days things were different. And my father was allowed to go up on that lift. He is not an adventurous man. But he took the risk of going on that scary-looking lift just to see the building construction.'

Valliappa is up to date on new trends in buildings and was quick to ensure that all his projects were green. 'Green buildings lead to healthier, happier and more productive lives,' he stresses. He believes workers in green and well-ventilated offices work more efficiently. All Sona buildings have airy, well-ventilated rooms with great views.

Whenever a building project has necessitated the felling of a tree on the Sona campus, Valliappa has ordered it to be transplanted. He personally monitors the transplanted tree, without considering the expenses.

His staff members describe how he goes to great lengths to look after trees and plants. A planter box in his home would keep flooding and ruining the floors. His well-wishers suggested he should remove the planter box. But he stubbornly retained the plant in its place, because as per Vastu the planter box was supposed to be at window level. Instead, he bent his mind to solve the problem of keeping it there without damage. The plant is blooming and thriving.

While most of Valliappa's commercial projects or office buildings have clean, contemporary lines, when it comes to his own residences, there is always a Chettinad influence. His house in Koramangala, today known as billionaire's street, has some of the magnificent carved wooden elements that evoke the beauty of the Chettinad palaces. The art on the wall are rich traditional pieces – Tanjore paintings and patachitras. Gorgeous statuettes of Lord Ganesha abound. There are Ravi Varma paintings.

'He picked up an interest in art, thanks to Karumuttu's influence,' says Chocko. 'Whenever Karumuttu came to Bengaluru, he would go to auction houses and often he would take me along,' says Valliappa.

Karumuttu had an impressive collection of heritage clock pieces. 'He had timeless timepieces that harked back to the Victorian era and which you would see in museums in London or Hyderabad,' says Chocko, who incidentally has a passion for horology and creates artistic clocks in his studio.

Valliappa says one of his favourite collector's items is an oval walnut tea table that he picked up at an auction he went to along with Karumuttu. 'Both my grandfather and I liked it immediately. But he generously told me to take it,' says Valliappa.

When his ancestral home in Poolankurichi was nearing its hundredth year, the bug of restoration bit Valliappa. He got the Bengaluru-based restoration architect and photographer Vikram Ponappa to restore the palatial home, lovingly spending time and resources to bring back the mansion to its old, glorious splendour. Everything, from the luxurious Belgian chandeliers, the exquisite vegetable oil paintings on the eggshell plaster walls and roofs, and stunning chequered Athangudi tiles, was restored painstakingly.

Simultaneously, under Valliappa's direction, Ponappa and the civil engineering team at Sona began restoring Valliappa's summer holiday home in Yercaud, a beautiful colonial-style bungalow in a 10-acre estate, situated on a rocky outcrop that gives it is name – Rocky Estate. A long, covered veranda facing the estate has been added to the front of the bungalow, adding more character even as it is being modernised with the addition of modern toilets, a dining room and more rooms.

The original four-bedroom bungalow is now a six-bedroom home with attached dressing rooms, toilets and powder rooms, and a dining and living room. The original structure had 20-inch-thick walls made up of random rocks held together by mud mortar. Ponappa's team added strength and structure to the outside by plastering with lime mortar. The electrical cables and sewage systems have been re-laid, and the roof tiles waterproofed. 'Both Chocko and Valliappa were very keen not to demolish the old bungalow because years ago Chocko had written a story in which the house played an important part,' says Ponappa. The estate grows coffee, with pepper in small pockets, and has a lot of shade-giving silver oak trees.

Water used to be a perennial problem here and when Ponappa suggested building a rainwater catchment tank, Valliappa was enthusiastically supportive. 'Now there is sufficient water and besides irrigating Rocky Estate there is also enough water to share with the neighbour, who needed it desperately,' says Ponappa.

The estate is more than a holiday home now. It's an integral part of the community and provides a creative outlet for the students at the Sona campus – for here is located the Sona FM Radio Tower.

The FM Tower is a pet project of Chocko, who nurtured dreams of being a radio jockey when he was young. He has now made it a meaningful venture by starting a community radio, which is located at the highest point on Rocky Estate.

Building the radio tower was easier said than done as it needed to be situated on a rocky outcrop with multiple levels. So Ponappa designed it using pre-engineered panels and steel.

'Valliappa visited the site as often as convenient to understand the situation on the ground. He went into the design details and suggested how we could improve on it,' says Ponappa. 'When we were looking at building the Sona FM tower, the first thing he suggested was to make a road to take materials up and this saved us time.'

Ponappa says that Valliappa taught him important lessons on cost-saving. 'Once we started the process of renovation at Rocky Estate bungalow, he taught me where to spend more and where to limit expenses. The earlier windows, though large, had several mullions or divisions, thereby inhibiting the view.

He suggested larger glass openings to open up the views to the estate. The dining area was small, and he showed me a structural wall that was holding up the roof, explained how it could be removed and how the roof could be supported in a different way, thereby creating a larger dining space.'

Ponappa says he never hesitates to take ideas to the Sona chairman. 'One thing about the chairman is that whenever I've approached him with an idea, however whacky and far-fetched it is, he will hear it out. He then weighs it from different angles – cost, impact on the space, sustainability, how useful it will be. He never dismisses it. He then suggests a workable solution. If he feels it's worth spending on, he approves the budget; otherwise he says, let's make a small working model and then explore the possibilities of expanding.'

Ponappa says that since Valliappa was interested and involved in architectural projects since he was nineteen, he's someone who got his hands and feet completely dirty to understand construction. 'With this kind of experience, he knows the potential of construction materials and how to design. Mix this with his business acumen and we have perfect cocktail of successful construction!'

Adhiyaman says that Valliappa is extremely strict about keeping the construction site clean – the instructions are not to leave loose nails lying around or any dangerous object hanging. He advises the construction contractors to remove debris from the site. Once a contractor was casual about the debris and Valliappa walked up to him and told him to have it removed. The man said he was waiting for his workers. This did not please Valliappa, whose philosophy is that no job is too mean to do oneself.

Says Adhiyaman, 'The chairman goes into micro details on every construction project. He not only enquires about delivery of the raw material but also checks the process of transportation and the time during which they are delivered. He encourages every faculty member and every student from the Department of Civil Engineering to look at buildings and architecture with new eyes. He persuades them to voice their opinions and innovative ideas as well.' Adhiyaman says that the construction of the new Sona College of Technology building took five years to complete – affected as it was by the lockdown brought on by the COVID-19 pandemic. In those five years, the chairman visited the site continuously. 'There is no place in the building without his footstep on it,' he says.

The foundations of the Sona campus may have been laid by his grandfather, and the building blocks put up by his father, but it's Valliappa who has given it shape and character and constructed an edifice to be proud of.

13

The Man and His Life Mantras

'**M**Y FATHER HAS no MBA degree but his management and leadership abilities are far superior to anything a school can teach,' says Thyagu Valliappa. These leadership skills have been honed by first observing and absorbing the working styles of his grandfather Karumuttu Thiagarajar and his father, Chockalingam. And then sixty years of hands-on working, navigating ups and downs in his businesses, has given him a unique outlook and philosophy on life.

Thyagu points out how his father, a BCom student without an engineering background, made a success of textile manufacturing business and, later, real estate. 'As he often says, the person who makes the plane cannot fly the plane. My father may not be able to use all the tools in a computer. But he knows how to get things done,' says Thyagu.

His biggest asset is he knows whom to ask, Thyagu adds. 'And he learns from all levels – from the students at Sona, from his driver, from his peers. It's what we call mirror management or reflective management.'

Those who have worked with Valliappa point to his gentle strength of purpose, his simplicity and lack of ego. Everyone also talks about his sharp memory and persistence. H. Shivarao, Sona Group's vice president of administration, who has been with the group for over forty years, says that if Valliappa gave him some instruction he was sure to follow up on it the next day. Even after a month, he would persistently ask him. 'He never forgets,' says Sivarao. 'He appreciates hard work, and rewards commensurately through bonuses. He knows how to make people happy.'

It may seem to people that he lives on a billionaires' street in Koramangla, but Valliappa points out with a mischievous twinkle in his eyes that he got there much before it became one. He chooses to drive a BMW because he considers it the safest and most comfortable transport given the amount he is on the road and it saves time too. 'I don't like to flaunt. At the same time, I don't sacrifice my comforts either,' he says.

Blessed with a dry wit, Valliappa's sense of humour is subtle. But it's his presence of mind and quick repartee that fills people with admiration. For instance, once he went to interact with the students at the Sona K-12 school. They were playing with gulmohar flowers and plucking the inner stalk which resembled an elephant. The talk turned to elephants and one of the kids asked Valliappa why an elephant is so big. Without batting an eyelid, he said, 'Because its mother and father are so big.'

In business dealings, one must consider things carefully before answering, says Valliappa. 'My grandfather used to say, if you want to gain time, tell a diversionary story, by which time you can think of a response.'

Vikram Ponappa, architect and now a close family friend, talks about the wonderful mentoring role that Valliappa has played. 'He taught me first-hand how to understand a situation when I was at crossroads. If it was design, it wasn't a solution he gave, but a thought process as to how one can solve it. If it was materials, he talked about which material to use and where it would make an impact.

'He also taught me how to negotiate to win – the foundation, the approach, the breakeven point and when to close. If it didn't work, he would tell me, "Leave it, we will revisit it later." My style of working is to have a notebook, make notes, sketch out a design. But the chairman's style is completely in his brain. He has a phenomenal memory for spaces, dimensions, cardinal directions and for the rules of Vastu. And he will state the solution in a way that one can visually understand,' he says.

Ponappa says another amazing quality of Valliappa is how he accommodates meeting times to suit the comfort of everyone. 'Recently we were to meet at Vee Plantations on Sunday, as he had a busy schedule. I requested him, if it's possible, could we please finish it by Saturday as I need to be home on Sunday. He rejigged his entire schedule to accommodate this request.'

Ask Valliappa about his business and life mantras, and these are what he spells out.

1) **Always think in the long term**
   There are many instances in Valliappa's life where he has taken decisions that seemed strange to others, but, as he explains, his vision is always long term. The land investments he made – be it the coffee estate or the parcel of land owned by a north Indian business group that came up during an auction – were all with an eye on the long term. He says, similarly, all his associations and relationships are long term. The architectural firm IMK Architects that worked with him on Sona Towers in the 1980s has continued working with him for over forty years and executes most of his projects. Ditto the furniture vendor at Sona Towers, Anand Joseph, who went on to do projects for the group. Says Joseph, 'Mr Valliappa helps budding entrepreneurs. He gave us our first assignment when he asked us to create furniture for an office at Sona Towers, and since then he has always been in touch asking us what is new in the market. He keeps himself updated and tends to go with the latest designs and trends.'
   During the COVID-19 pandemic, a leading tile maker and supplier to the group approached Valliappa,

explaining that he was facing severe financial difficulties. The supplier proposed selling tiles at a 50 per cent discount if Valliappa provided an advance of ₹1 crore. Recognising the importance of supporting a partner in distress, Valliappa promptly signed a cheque, thereby helping to save a vendor on the brink of collapse. The supplier not only fulfilled the order in the following months but also repaid the advance. This exemplifies how Valliappa thrives by building relationships founded on trust.

2) **Influence without being bossy**
It's not in Valliappa's nature to issue a command or directive. Instead, he will discuss an issue threadbare and listen to all points. But in the end, most people who have done business with him say that he manages to convince people about what he wants. 'He leads without being bossy,' says a faculty member at Sona.

3) **Always be positive**
'When he comes into the office, he always enters with a smile and in a positive mood and motivates people,' says Shivarao. Life has dealt Valliappa with many challenges, but he doesn't like to dwell on these. His advice to everyone is to look on the positive side. And to say yes to things: one should attempt and fail rather than not giving it a go. 'Saying yes opens you up to new challenges and opportunities. If you wait until you feel ready to pursue an opportunity, chances are it will pass you by. Saying yes means that you are open to moving past your comfort zone and embracing a new challenge,' he says.

It's this attitude, Valliappa says, that allowed him to move ahead when the textile businesses declined to a point of no return. 'I could have easily sold the mill land and retired. But I started something new,' he says.

4) **Keep your books in order and borrow only that which you can pay back**
Valliappa's outlook on finance is very disciplined. He believes in taking debt to start businesses or to scale ventures, but he is careful not to over-borrow. 'You must borrow only as much as you have the capacity to pay back. I make sure I pay very promptly.' Having once been scalded, and also seen how many family businesses are in trouble, he cannot stress enough about not overstretching. At the same time, he takes bold gambles on land, investing widely.

When it comes to running his businesses, he spends a lot on a few areas he deems critical, such as skilling of staff and employee welfare, or on latest technology, but he is extremely particular about wastage. 'His instruction is that not one nail should be thrown away loosely. He understands the value of each item,' says a staff member.

5) **Pay attention to detail**
Although not a micromanager, Valliappa is big on attention to detail. For instance, he is particular about the furniture in the Sona classrooms. He believes that correct posture contributes a lot to a student's concentration and learning. So he personally tests the furniture he commissions by sitting on it. If the desk hits his knees when his feet are placed on the footrest, he tells the carpenters to modify the table. He waxes eloquent about how the students' knees should not be above 90 degrees for optimal alignment, and thus the positioning of the foot support is important. 'We make furniture for our group requirements in the workshop,' says Adhiyaman. 'In the guest house at the Sona College, where the chairman

resides whenever he visits the college, he has insisted that his bed and other furniture items should be the same as those used by students in the hostels, so that he knows whether they are comfortable or not.'

6) **Health is wealth. Take breaks to unwind**
Every year, Valliappa makes it a point to go on a ten-day rejuvenation holiday to a wellness resort. 'I have been to Jindal, Shaukya and several Kerala Ayurveda resorts,' he says. The greatest wealth is health, he stresses. His wife, Seetha Aachi, says he hardly takes any fried items and his favourite snack is a steamed preparation. Peppery soups and thin buttermilk, which he has before lunch and dinner, are a source of energy.

7) **Always be curious**
Valliappa is a lifelong learner. He says that continuous learning has an intrinsic value in professional development. One of his businesses – a diversion into copper sulphate – came about because of his desire to learn. He got excited when Professor Rajinder Kumar described the process and set up the business. Once, a business acquaintance in Bengaluru told him about a new type of water heater. Excited that it could be used in the Sona campus, he at once enquired all the details about it and then invited all the principals, heads of various departments, faculty members of the electrical department and hostel wardens to understand the working method of the unusual water heater.

Whenever he encountered a new piece of machinery or technology, he would at once want it to be shared in the institute. The mechanical engineering faculty remembers how Valliappa once got excited about a compressed air energy storage (CAES) system and introduced it to the engineering students, urging them to try their hands on it. Similarly, when he heard about an automated groundwater recycling system, he quickly bought it for the Sona campus despite the cost (it was over ₹6 lakh). He saw twin benefits of getting one: it would be useful for rainwater harvesting and the students could experiment with it and come up with new technologies in this area.

8) Share the knowledge

Every time he learns about a new technology or visits an interesting place Valliappa is eager to share the details. But he does not stop at mere verbal retelling. When he visited the Bosch Museum near Bengaluru, he was so captivated that he wanted to introduce a similar museum in his institution. He at once arranged for five of his faculty members to visit the museum, defraying all the expenses. When the faculty members returned from the museum trip, Valliappa was eagerly waiting for them at the campus to get their reaction and feedback. But curbing his impatience, he first ensured they had something to eat and only then asked about their views on museum. That totally endeared him to the faculty.

9) Be accessible to everyone

At the Sona College any student or parent can go and meet the chairman, who believes in being accessible to all. So has he met all the students at the college? 'Only the good ones and the struggling ones,' he responds with a twinkle. 'The good ones come to me to get their photograph clicked with me when they bag a prize or achieve something. The struggling students come to me for guidance and help.'

He recounts the case of a student who had scored 198 out of 200 and yet could not get a placement. He would give interview after interview with companies that had come for placement to Sona but failed to get an offer. So Valliappa intervened, calling him to his office to motivate him and prepare him for the next interview. The student aced the next interview and got a job.

Principal Kadhar Nawaz recounts how Sunil Kumar K., topper of the Tamil Nadu Common Entrance Test (TANCET), sought admission to the Master of Computer Applications programme at Sona College of Technology in 2011. 'When I informed Valliappa about Sunil's brilliance and dedication despite being visually challenged by birth, he was deeply moved and immediately offered all necessary assistance, including a hundred per cent scholarship,' says Khadar Nawaz.

Sunil Kumar, now a senior manager with Bank of Baroda, often returns to Sona College of Arts and Science to deliver inspirational talks to students. Whenever he visits, he makes it a point to call on Valliappa and pay his respects.

10) **Be kind and humble. Never yield to egoism. Forgive and forget.**
Valliappa is not given to holding grudges. As he says, his darkest moment was when his brother kept him away from his mother and had disagreements over property. But years later when his brother was ailing and in hospital all alone, it was Valliappa who went to take care of him. When he passed away, he arranged the funeral in befitting style.
Similarly, when Dhiraj Lal, a former principal of the Sona College of Technology opened a rival college in Salem, and invited Valliappa to visit, his children were baffled when he not only visited the college but inaugurated the proceedings.

14

Looking Ahead: Entrepreneurs, Not Inheritors

STUDY AFTER STUDY on family businesses has shown that less than 4 per cent of them survive beyond the fourth generation. There is a much-talked-about third-generation curse on family businesses.

Thyagu Valliappa, who is the fourth generation of the Sona Group, however, thinks that his father has managed to break the curse.

'Perhaps we were blessed to have gone through a terribly rough patch. If we had not faced the difficulties we did over the textile business, probably things would have been different for us,' he reflects. The closure of the textile business forced the family to look at other businesses and the timing – at the cusp of India's liberalisation – was right for new enterprises to take off.

He also feels that since each generation in the group – be it Karumuttu, Chockalingam, Valliappa or Chocko and him – has behaved like a first-generation businessman and not like an inheritor, things have panned out differently for them.

'Karumuttu may have passed down the textile mill to Chockalingam, but my grandfather also created his own enterprises, as did my father,' he says. 'Now Chocko has his own start-ups, as do I.'

When Chockalingam passed away, the transition was not smooth. He had three sons, but the middle son died at a young age. After consulting with his wife, Meenakshi Aachi,

Looking Ahead: Entrepreneurs, Not Inheritors

Chockalingam decided to leave the mill in Salem to his son Sundaram, the house in Salem to Valliappa and divide the Sona Towers and the Sona educational setups between the two sons. 'Meenakshi Aachi felt that Rajendra Mills and the house in Salem had come to Chockalingam through her father and as such she had a say in how it was to be divided,' says Chocko.

As fate would have it, things did not pan out according to Chockalingam's and Meenakshi Aachi's wishes. But Sundaram and his family could not retain the Salem house which they had taken over. The mill business they inherited ran into difficulties.

Having seen so much acrimony in the division of the family businesses, Valliappa was keen to split his own businesses between his sons during his lifetime.

In 2016–17, Valliappa got all his businesses valued professionally, and he divided them equally between himself and his two sons. All three have a pie in Sona Education, with Valliappa the chairman, and Chocko and Thyagu vice chairmen. With the education institutions, each brother carved out his own niche.

Thyagu got the Lalbagh plantations and the Sona Valliappa Textile Mill in Salem. He had his own Play factory enterprise that he started up, and Sona Ayush, a health and wellness initiative.

Chocko got Vee Technologies with Valliappa being a 25 per cent shareholder in the company.

Both Chocko and Thyagu are building future focused businesses – Vee Tech has seven verticals in emerging areas, while Thyagu has bet on health and wellness, and building management apps, among other things.

Valliappa is waiting for his grandson Varun to complete his studies and join him to scale his real estate business. 'He will look after business development and marketing. I need a hand to help me grow the business,' says Valliappa.

The Sona Story

With Chocko and Thyagu helping him, he is scaling up on Sona's education offerings too, with a Sona Nursing College in the offing. The land purchased from a large industrial group in Salem will be used for the expansion of Sona into the healthcare space. 'We will start with paramedical training first, and then alternative medicine,' says Valliappa.

Meanwhile, Chocko is focused on growing Vee Technologies. 'Ten years ago I took a decision to organise my business in a warp and weft format. The seven verticals form the warp, and the weft is all the administrative, finance, marketing and HR functions,' he explains.

The seven verticals are Vee Tech (IT Services), Vee Healthtek (medical coding, revenue cycle management of hospitals and analytics), Vee Create (design), Vee AEC (Architectural Engineering and Construction), Vee Govern (eGovernance backend like Aadhaar enrolments), Vee Move (logistics software) and Vee Animation (E-learning).

Vee Tech's healthcare vertical works with over 150 US hospitals, including six of the top ten healthcare systems, helping them handle clinical coding and revenue cycle management services. It also works with insurance companies in the US with a new-age Medicare plan that incentivises people to stay healthy. Insurers make money if people don't have to go to hospitals. Sitting in Bengaluru, Salem, Hyderabad, Trichy and Chennai, Vee Tech's coders look at patient data and use analytics to figure out the chances of getting an ailment cured and suggesting interventions to prevent a major illness.

Some of the other verticals have interesting origin stories. For instance, Vee AEC came into being because someone accidentally dropped a cup of coffee on Chocko's shoe. 'I was at a conference and one guy accidentally spilled coffee on my shoe. We got talking and I learnt his name was Tarun Mirchandani, better known as Tony Mirchandani. He said he was into engineering design. I said, so am I. He said, "I run an MEP firm." I asked him what an MEP was and he said mechanical, electrical and plumbing. I told him I do mechanical. We design fire trucks for US towns. If you see a fire truck in the US, there is a 30 per cent chance it is designed by us.' Every zip code in the US has a different legislation and the truck design depends on the zipcode. Some zipcodes have lot of high-rise buildings so you need trucks with long ladders. Others are mid-rises and low villas, many are made with wood, some geographies the houses are made with stone. So the fire truck equipment depends on that.

Chocko persuaded Tony to have lunch with him. Things moved rapidly after that. Tony's firm RTM Associates had acquired fifty companies. He had a company in Baroda, but that office could not do design. So Tony came to Bengaluru to see Chocko's work, and a deal was sewn.

That was in 2018. By 2024, Vee AEC had become one of the leading MEP firms in the world.

If Chocko has been getting business from the US, Thyagu has been trialling interesting innovations out of the Sona campus.

Among other things, Thyagu is working on reducing paper at the Sona campus. A lot of it again is using technology to impressive uses. 'By 2026, the college will be completely paperless,' he says, describing the huge savings this will accrue to the institution as well as the carbon footprint it will reduce. 'Crores worth of paper will be saved, litres of water and hundreds of trees saved from being cut,' adds Thyagu.

Other benefits of going totally digital, he says, is that you get a lot of analytics. When you go digital, you also reduce correction time. Productivity and quality go up, he says.

In 2022, after the COVID-19 pandemic, seeing the increased need for healthcare, Thyagu began the Sona Ayush Clinic within the Sona campus. From yoga to naturopathy, the clinic offers a range of alternative care for total rejuvenation and rehabilitation. He also initiated plans to start Sona Medical College, a dream of his father. In 2022, Thyagu started Sona Star and TrackMySona, an app that allows efficient building and asset management.

The Valliappas are passionate about community projects and stay up to date with all the latest trends and technology.

The eminent scientist Muthu Krishnan, who has taken on the responsibility of driving Vee Healthtek's digital technology, says, 'Looking at the vision of the company, it's clear that technology is going to anchor the next era of its growth.' Rather perceptively he says, 'As a company they have always looked at problem-solving to create business value. And this spirit percolates everywhere. I really love the fact that they have invested so much in colleges and are creating the talent that can become the feeder for the growth of their companies. Look at the problems the students and faculty are already solving. It amazes me that from such a small city so much is coming out.'

Chocko agrees that problem-solving is in the genes of the group. 'I used to sit in the admin reviews and listen to people complaining about a bad smell. It was traced to toilets. That has given us a solution and a patent on preventing smells before it can spread. So, as I tell people, it's problems that lead to innovations.'

Valliappa chips in by saying that if there is no problem, then everybody will be able to do everything. Only if there are problems will it separate the ones who can achieve something from others.

Summing up, it is a group that thrives on taking challenges and motivation to scale up.

Acknowledgements

THIS BOOK WOULD NOT have been written without the tremendous help of the faculty at the Department of English at Sona College of Arts and Science. They kickstarted the project, under the guidance of principal G.M. Kadhar Nawaz, doing the initial research and interviews, and even created a rough outline.

Grateful thanks to Dr G. Anuradha, Dr R. Pavithra, S. Preethi Shalina and Dr M. Aravindh for their tremendous work.

Special thanks also to architect Vikram Ponappa and M. Adhiyaman who contributed immensely to the chapters on architecture. A mention must be made of Sona College's photographer J. Senthil Kumar, who sifted through pictures and helped with the photographs.

At Sona Towers, H. Shivarao, who has been with the group for a long time, was an invaluable help, not only arranging meetings with key people but also recalling crucial incidents.

Heartfelt gratitude also to the friends, family, colleagues, business associates and well-wishers of Mr Valliappa, who took time out to share anecdotes and stories that enriched the book.

Notes

1 Under the Banyan Tree

1. Montek Singh Ahluwalia, 'Rajiv Gandhi Opened the Doors for 1991 Reforms', *The Week*, 30 May 2021, https://www.theweek.in/theweek/cover/2021/05/20/rajiv-gandhi-opened-the-doors-for-1991-reforms--montek-singh-ahl.html

2 The Nagarathar Way: The Chettiar Heritage

1. 'Chettinad's Legacy', *Frontline*, https://frontline.thehindu.com/arts-and-culture/heritage/article25547717.ece
2. https://www.scribd.com/document/52838424/History-of-Nattukottai-Nagarathar
3. https://www.scribd.com/document/52838424/History-of-Nattukottai-Nagarathar
4. 'Chettinad's Legacy', *Frontline*, https://frontline.thehindu.com/arts-and-culture/heritage/article25547717.ece
5. Radha Thiagarajan, *Karumuttu Thiagaraja Chettiar: The Textile King* (Vanathi Pathikppakam, 2004)

6 Vyaparam: The 'Can Do' Spirit

1. TNN, 'Hejjala Firing: Report Blames Police', *The Times of India*, 22 January 2002, https://timesofindia.indiatimes.com/city/bengaluru/hejjala-firing-report-blames-police/articleshow/1282282768.cms